Fourth Edition

Emma Shinn

Accounting and Financial Management

For Residential Construction

BuilderBooks™
National Association of Home Builders
1201 15th Street, NW
Washington, DC 20005-2800
www.builderbooks.com

Accounting and Financial Management
for Residential Construction
Emma Shinn

ISBN 0-86718-534-1

Cover design by Armen Kojoyian
Printed in the United States of America

Library of Congress Cataloging-in-Publication Data

Shinn, Emma S.
    Accounting and financial management for residential construction / by
Emma Shinn.— 4th ed.
        p. cm.
Rev. ed. of: Accounting and financial management for builders,
remodelers, and developers. 3rd ed. c1993.
Includes bibliographical references and index.
    ISBN 0-86718-534-1 (pbk.)
    1. Construction industry—United States—Accounting. 2. Managerial
accounting—United States. I. Title.
    HF5686.B7 S54 2002
    657'.869—dc21
                              2002010829

Disclaimer
This publication is designed to provide accurate and authoritative information
in regard to the subject matter covered. It is sold with the understanding that the
publisher is not engaged in rendering legal, accounting, or other professional
service. If legal advice or other expert assistance is required, the services of a
competent professional person should be sought.
—From a Declaration of Principles jointly adopted by a Committee of the
American Bar Association and a Committee of Publishers and Associations.

For further information, please contact:
BuilderBooks™
National Association of Home Builders
1201 15th Street, NW
Washington, DC 20005-2800
(800) 223-2665
Check us out online at: www.builderbooks.com

08/02 SLR Production Service / Data Reproduction Corp. 1500

About the Author

Emma Shinn of Lee Evans Group / IHBMI, Littleton, Colorado, is a consultant and educator for the homebuilding industry in accounting and financial management systems. In the 1960s she worked for Touche, Ross, and Company (now Deloitte & Touche). She has an MBA in accounting from The American University in Washington, D.C., and is a certified public accountant (CPA). She helped draft the first *Builder's Cost of Doing Business Study* conducted by the National Association of Home Builders. She served as Chairman of the NAHB Business Management and Information Technology Committee in 1997.

Her background in the industry includes all aspects of the building process including planning, design, supervision, sales and administration of single family projects. She was awarded the MAME award for the Rookie Salesperson of the Year by the Denver Home Builders Association in 1988. Emma's specialization is accounting for the homebuilding industry, addressing not only financial reporting but also the use of accounting information in the management process.

Acknowledgments

Accounting and Financial Management for Residential Construction is the product of several years of planning, writing, and reviewing by people concerned with improving the management of homebuilding, remodeling, and land development firms.

Special credit is due to Lee S. Evans of Lee S. Evans and Associates, Inc., Nederland, Colorado, who developed the original NAHB Chart of Accounts. The NAHB Financial Management Issues Work Group of the Business Management & Information Technology Committee has updated the Chart of Accounts again for this edition.

Many thanks to the following individuals who contributed their time and expertise to reviewing the manuscript for *Accounting and Financial Management for Residential Construction:* Steve Hays, Partner, Rubin, Brown, Gornstein & Company, St. Louis, Missouri, and Steve Maltzman, President, Steve Maltzman and Associates, Redlands, California.

The author would also like to thank those individuals who contributed their time and expertise to reviewing the previous editions: Greg Caruso, President, Caruso Homes, Crofton, Maryland; Ken Waetzman, President, Waetzman Realty Advisors, Cherry Hill, New Jersey; and Jamie Wolf, President, Wolfworks, Farmington, Connecticut.

Accounting and Financial Management for Residential Construction was produced under the general direction of Gerald Howard, NAHB Executive Vice President and CEO, in association with NAHB staff members Michael Shibley, Executive Vice President, Builder, Associate & Affiliate Services; Greg French, Staff Vice President, Publications and Non-dues Revenues; Eric Johnson, Publisher, BuilderBooks; Theresa Minch, Executive Editor, and Jessica Poppe, Assistant Editor.

Contents

Chapter 15

Appendix A

Appendix B

Appendix C

Appendix D

Appendix E

Appendix F

Appendix G

Figure List

Foreword

The National Association of Home Builders believes that the performance and profitability of its members, regardless of the size of their businesses, can be enhanced by the use of standardized accounting procedures. By regularly using a financial reporting system, builders, remodelers, and developers can determine their financial position at any time.

The use of standardized financial reporting also permits each of them to measure his or her firm's current performance against (a) its records for previous years, (b) the performance of other builders, and (c) the industry itself. In addition the collection of financial information in a standardized format creates a historical database that enhances the budget and planning functions.

This revised and expanded fourth edition of *Accounting and Financial Management for Residential Construction* includes the complete, updated NAHB Chart of Accounts.

This book tells you how to—
* Understand bookkeeping and accounting terminology and procedures
* Design an accounting system and choose an accountant
* Do financial planning and job cost accounting
* Prepare, analyze, and use information generated by an accounting system
* Adopt and use financial tools that pinpoint deviation from your company's plan or budget
* Create confidence in a firm's financial statements among financial institutions, sureties, and local, state, and federal agencies

Accounting and Financial Management also includes the job cost control subsidiary ledger accounts for direct, indirect, and land development costs. This publication can be used by any type of builder (single family, multifamily or commercial), remodeler, developer, or subcontractor.

This book does not purport to cover every possible accounting technique or problem, nor is it intended to replace consultation with an accountant or tax advisor.

Introduction

A universal accounting system for all builders is not possible because each system must reflect the financial transactions and management philosophy of the individual builder. *Accounting and Financial Management for Residential Construction* offers guidelines and a general structure for designing an accounting system on the assumption that the reader has no previous knowledge of accounting. It presents an overview of accounting theory that will provide an understanding of how an accounting system operates and what basic principles are followed in the processing of financial data.

Accounting and Financial Management addresses:
- Choosing an accountant
- General concepts and various methods of processing data
- Principles and guidelines for setting up the structure of an accounting system
- Procedures for recording and processing financial data in the system and for generating reports from the system
- Procedures for analyzing financial statements and data accumulated by the system
- Job cost accounting system
- Financial planning and development of budgets
- Guidelines for preparing budgets
- Use of planning as an integral part of the control function of an accounting system

CHAPTER I

Designing the System and Choosing an Accountant

Traditionally, accounting has focused on its reporting responsibilities to third parties versus reporting to managers or internal users and, understandably so, because of the professional liability attached to submitting erroneous information to third parties. As a general rule, third parties rely on financial reports to make decisions that would place their capital at risk. Therefore, if the reports are not accurate, third parties can sustain personal losses. In other instances, reports are submitted to third parties to comply with regulatory agencies or taxing authorities. Accuracy of the information is, again, of the essence for these users. In both of these instances, however, the users have no need for a lot of detail. These users like to classify accounting information in very broad categories to facilitate an overview analysis of the operations and the financial strength of the company. They are evaluating the profitability of the business, not analyzing where profits are coming from or what areas could be improved to increase profits.

Because of the emphasis on third-party reporting, it is not unusual to have accountants neglect to view the accounting information and function as a management tool. The accounting system holds incredible amounts of data because it measures each economic activity that takes place in the company. It is like the blood system of a company because it touches every department and function within. It can potentially provide managers at every level of the organization with critical information to better run each functional area of the company and evaluate past performance. Yet this system is probably the most ignored source of information in a homebuilding organization.

Accounting is the process of collecting, analyzing, classifying, and accumulating historical financial transactions in categories and formats that will accurately reflect a company's operation and present its financial position. The set up of the system is critical to the types of reports and amount of detail it will generate. Therefore, managers need to participate in planning the design of the system by identifying the type of information and level of detail they would like to have available to manage functional areas more effectively.

The accounting system should be designed not as a tax system or to meet the requirements of third-party users but as a management system to meet management needs. Such a system can be converted easily to meet the requirements of third-party users. The same is not true if the system is designed as a tax system. It is time-consuming and in some instances almost impossible to prepare detailed reports from a system set up primarily to support tax and third-party requirements.

Why should the builder, remodeler, or developer worry about accounting at all? Through the accounting function you can obtain timely financial information that will make the decision-making process less of a guessing game. Accounting records contain a wealth of historical information that can be used effectively to:

- Analyze past performance
- Evaluate the financial strength of your company
- Evaluate the feasibility of future projects
- Estimate the cost of future jobs
- Set goals and objectives
- Prepare short- and long-term budgets

Accounting also provides the framework for the control system. The basis of any control system is to measure performance and compare it to goals and objectives previously set up by the company. Accounting provides the means to measure performance and the structure to accumulate the measurements into meaningful classifications.

Key to any control system is the development of goals and objectives in quantitative terms. Once again, accounting provides the framework to set up the plans and objectives in financial terms and to allow for easy comparison between plan and actual performance.

Planning and controlling are just two of the five basic management functions, which consist of:

- Planning
- Organizing
- Staffing
- Directing
- Controlling

As a management tool, accounting plays a key role in both planning and controlling. However, builders, remodelers, and developers are constantly underestimating this key resource that is already a part of their organization. They need to recognize the tremendous impact of utilizing this tool in the management of their companies because it allows them to:

- Make decisions based on facts versus just gut feeling
- Know where the company stands on an on-going basis and eliminate year-end surprises
- Make informed decisions when allocating resources to new ventures
- Have better lead times to react to adverse conditions
- Measure the performance of the different functional areas of the company such as construction, financing, sales and marketing, and general administration
- Measure the performance of different communities or subdivisions
- Provide a historical basis and the road map for developing future plans and budgets
- Support documentation to defend a position to lenders and investors
- Obtain objective information to engage in better negotiations with vendors and subcontractors

- Obtain objective information to work towards elimination of waste, cost variances, and inefficiencies in company operations

Don't underestimate the power of a good accounting system in the management of day-to-day operations. But remember that it goes beyond the traditional set of financial statements prepared to satisfy lender and governmental requirements.

Designing the System

A successful accounting system starts, like a house, remodeling job, or new subdivision, with design. Therefore, the following steps require special attention:

- Take a good look at your firm's organizational structure. Is it a sole proprietorship, a partnership, a C corporation, or an S corporation? Reporting requirements differ under each structure.
- Analyze all functions carried out within the organization and who is responsible for each function. Prepare an organizational chart that shows each function in a hierarchy and the names of individuals responsible for carrying out each function. In a small firm one individual might be responsible for more than one function. In larger organizations each function might be broken down into sub-functional areas, each staffed by a different person. Larger organizations usually need to sort financial information using a larger number of classifications or accounts to be able to get reports with more detail than those needed by smaller organizations. Therefore, an organization's size has an impact on the types of reports it will need to generate, making the accounting systems more complex for larger organizations than for smaller ones.
- Make projections about future growth and determine the effects it will have on resources and staff as production increases. Can your present staff handle the additional time demands and increased responsibilities? Will you need to add staff? How much authority and responsibility should you delegate to other employees? These projections must be carefully done because the size of your company impacts the design of the accounting system, specifically the amount of detail that will be generated from the system

and the points of control required within the system.

- Determine the type of reports you would want the system to generate. Design the reports and determine the frequency, users, and how much detail should be included in the report. Determining the output (the reports) of the accounting system at the design stage allows for efficient and timely preparation of the reports. Once the system has been designed, major revisions to reports might require changes in the system's basic structure. Any changes to an existing system can be disruptive and thwart the capabilities of the system while implementing the changes.

Under no circumstances should an accountant or consultant design an accounting system without the active participation of the builder, remodeler, or developer. For larger firms, the top management team must participate in the design process. It is through the owners' and managers' participation that the system will perform effectively and be able to satisfy the organization's needs and requirements.

Beware when buying computer software. The software provides the mechanism to process the information, not the structure for processing the data. If you are looking at software that offers a predesign structure to run the accounting system, make sure that the structure will meet your management needs because in most cases it will not.

Choosing An Accountant

An accounting system involves two levels of attention: professional and technical or clerical. Certified public accountants (CPAs) and accountants provide the professional input and bookkeepers and clerical personnel provide the data entry and processing. The difference between an accountant and a CPA is primarily one of approach and who the person works for. The CPA, a member of an independent accounting firm, is primarily concerned with the validity of financial information because third parties are the primary users. The independent CPA provides some form of assurance that the financial statements are not materially misstated. In contrast, the accountant is usually a company employee who may also have CPA credentials. The accountant works with the accounting information from the management perspective, maintains internal controls, prepares the traditional financial statements as well as management reports, and helps analyze the reports. Bear in mind that the financial function (reporting to third parties) and the managerial function (reporting to managers) of accounting are not in conflict. In fact, today many CPA firms offer their clients both services on a consultation basis.

CPAs use universal principles and standards established by the American Institute of Certified Public Accountants (AICPA) board, commonly known as Generally Accepted Accounting Principles (GAAP), to determine whether the financial statements represent fairly a company's financial position. They require little specialized knowledge from industry to industry. In contrast, the processing and evaluation of financial information for management use requires extensive knowledge of each industry. Therefore, not all CPA firms can provide the expertise needed to design and implement a system that will serve both as the source for external reporting and as a management tool in the daily decision-making process of a homebuilding company.

The job cost system is an important element in the accounting system for a homebuilding, remodeling, or development company. At least 50 percent of the charges against sales revenue are construction costs, thus representing the biggest single line item affecting a firm's profitability. The job cost system operates as a subsidiary system of the general accounting system and accumulates cost not only by unit of production but also by cost code (lumber, plumbing, electric) within each unit. The unit might be a house, a remodeling job, a subdivision, or a commercial establishment. This subsidiary system establishes the framework for controlling construction cost.

The treatment of land, development costs, and indirect construction cost (including capitalization of interest) requires special attention for builders, remodelers, and developers. When accounting for land and land development costs, special capitalization rules must be followed. For indirect costs the structure to accumulate and control the costs as

well as the procedure to allocate those costs between sold and inventory units must be addressed.

When setting up the accounting system, management use of the financial information should be the primary consideration. However, attention should also be given to Internal Revenue Service regulations so that data is accumulated and classified for easy retrieval of information needed for tax purposes at the end of the year. Otherwise, time-consuming analysis and research might be required to be able to extract the required information. Because regulations change often, both you and your accountant must understand the latest regulations.

The Bookkeeper

Bookkeepers and clerical personnel are generally in charge of collecting, classifying, and accumulating financial information within a framework designed by an accountant. The daily handling of financial information is clerical in nature and can be easily handled in-house by a secretary or bookkeeper or outside by a bookkeeping service or a bookkeeping division of a CPA office. In some small-volume companies the builder, remodeler, developer, or an office manager may perform the bookkeeping duties. The bookkeeper's job is to collect and process data. Bookkeepers are not substitutes for accountants. They perform a necessary and valuable function in the accounting duties but they cannot perform a function for which they have not been trained. The accountant retains the responsibility for performing reviews for accuracy, analyzing the data, preparing reports, and reviewing the data collection process.

If you need to use an outside bookkeeping service, choose a service familiar with the homebuilding or remodeling industry. The bookkeeping service should follow the system and requirements designed by an accountant rather than some predetermined general requirement set by the service. The accountant should perform a monthly or, at a minimum, quarterly review of the bookkeeping function to ensure it is being performed accurately. The accountant is also responsible for preparing financial statements, special reports, and analytical reviews of the accounting information.

If the owner of a homebuilding, remodeling, or development company does not have enough accounting background to set up the firm's accounting system, the owner will need the design services of an accountant with some experience in homebuilding, remodeling, development, or at least construction accounting.

The Accountant

Selecting an accountant is a critical task for management, particularly in the building, remodeling, and land development industries because of the special requirements of each of these groups. For example, as stated earlier, job cost must be an integral part of the accounting system. The treatment and allocation of indirect construction cost also must meet special requirements for homebuilding, remodeling, or land development companies. The accountant needs to understand these processes as well as be sensitive to the company's management needs. Check references from other builders, remodelers, or developers who have used or are using the accountant. Attorneys are generally a good source to provide a reference to a qualified accountant.

Because specialization in the accounting profession is less likely in small towns, you may need to go to a nearby larger town to find a qualified accountant. At the least you would want to present your accountant with a copy of this manual as a guide to the specific requirements of the homebuilding, remodeling, and land development industries. As soon as size permits, hire an in-house accountant.

The Certified Public Accountant

For many small companies an in-house accountant is not a practical option and in some cases is unnecessary. The selection of a CPA is thus critical. The CPA should not only satisfy all traditional external requirements for reporting but also help management analyze financial information for controlling the business and making educated business decisions. Under these circumstances the CPA should have an in-depth knowledge of the homebuilding (not just construction) industry, the structure and organization of the individual company, its products and/or services, and construction methods.

Builder, remodelers, and developers must educate their CPAs in their company's internal operations and, in turn, be receptive to the CPA's recommendations and suggestions. A two-way dialogue is essential to the relationship between the builder, remodeler, or developer and the CPA. Above all, the right CPA can make the difference between a business that merely functions and one that prospers. Some companies will use the services of a CPA only for taxes. Other companies will engage the services of a CPA for audits, reviews, or compilations.

CPA Firms and Levels of Services Available

Generally, CPA firms offer three levels of services to their clients: audits, reviews, and compilations. Many CPA firms also provide management consulting services. The scope of the work done by a CPA firm will determine the type of service and the cost of the work performed.

Audits

An audit is by far the most comprehensive and expensive of the services offered by a CPA firm. After conducting the audit, the CPA firm will issue an opinion about the company's financial statements. Bear in mind that financial statements are representations made by management. The CPA merely offers an opinion as to whether the statements represent fairly the financial position of the company in accordance with GAAP.

The audit process includes verification of certain accounts by confirming bank balances, outstanding receivables, and accounts payable with the appropriate third parties. The CPA firm also scrutinizes the system of internal control to ensure the existence of and compliance with rules and procedures. The review of the financial information must be thorough enough to satisfy the CPA that the information presented in the financial statements accurately represents the financial condition of the company in accordance with GAAP or other consistently recognized system of accounting. Investors and lenders often require audits as a condition for loans or to invest capital. To save the expense of a detailed audit, builders, remodelers, and developers will often negotiate the removal of that requirement from financial documents.

Reviews

Audits are relatively expensive; therefore, companies not required by third parties to have audits often choose a less comprehensive service. A review provides a limited analysis or testing of the financial information. The opinion expressed after a review therefore is limited in scope because it generally does not include confirmation of account balances by third parties.

Because of the reduced scope of work, the cost of a review is less than that of an audit but more than a compilation. Many lenders require borrowers to provide annual statements that have been reviewed by a CPA firm. Reviews also provide a company's owners with limited assurance that the accounting department is following accepted procedures in the recording and reporting functions.

Compilations

Compilations are by far the least expensive of the three services offered by CPA firms. In a compilation the CPA is under no obligation to review or investigate any account or procedure unless something looks suspicious or appears to be misleading.

In a compilation the CPA issues no opinion as to the accuracy of the data. The CPA simply presents the data supplied by the management in an accepted financial format for disclosure to lenders, for income tax purposes, or for any other use intended by the owner.

Regardless of the service performed by the CPA, the financial statements are representations made by the homebuilding, remodeling, or development company. Ultimately, the company, not the CPA, is responsible for preparing the financial statements accurately.

CHAPTER 2

Basics of Accounting

T he purpose of this chapter is to eliminate some of the mystery surrounding accounting, not to make an accountant or bookkeeper of the reader. By gaining an understanding of the mechanics of accounting and the information it can generate through well-designed management reports you will find that your accounting system can be a highly effective management tool.

Accounting Systems

Financial data generated by a builder's, remodeler's, or developer's business operations should be classified, accumulated, and summarized following generally accepted accounting principles (GAAP). Any accounting system as a general rule has two tracks: financial and managerial. The financial track of the accounting system is general in nature (Figure 2–1). The managerial accounting system classifies data from the financial track into a more detailed structure for use in control and decision making.

	Main System Financial Accounting	Subsystem Managerial Accounting
Nature	General	Detail
Structure	General Ledger	Subsidiary Ledgers

Output	Financial Statement:
	  Income Statement
	  Balance Sheet
		Management Reports:
		  Cost Reports
		  Gross Profit Reports

Figure 2-1. Nature, Structure, and Output of an Accounting System

Financial Accounting System

The financial system maintains the overview of all financial transactions. The traditional financial statements, income statement, and balance sheet are prepared from information generated from the financial system.

Financial transactions are classified into the following categories or types of accounts:

- Assets
- Liabilities
- Owners' equity
- Revenues
- Expenses

Managerial Accounting System

The managerial accounting system includes a number of subsystems, also known as subsidiaries or detailed ledger systems. A managerial accounting system could include these subsidiaries:

- Material inventory
- Job cost for land development
- Job cost for work in process
- Finished lots
- Accounts receivable
- Accounts payable
- Construction loans payable

Figure 2–2 illustrates the flow of accounting data through the system, the relationship between fi-nancial and managerial accounting, and the output generated from each. Each subsidiary ledger in the managerial accounting system contains a detailed breakdown of an account in the general ledger or financial accounting system.

For example, the accounts payable subsidiary shows amounts currently owed each supplier and subcontractor, whereas the general ledger shows in one lump sum the amount owed to all suppliers and subcontractors. The total of all individual accounts in the subsidiary ledger must agree with the balance on the accounts payable account in the general ledger. This is critical to be able to validate the integrity and accuracy of the accounting information. The accounts payable account in the general ledger serves as a control account.

The job cost subsidiary works in a similar fashion. The general ledger account supporting the subsidiary is the work in process account. As in the case with accounts payable, the work in process account shows no details as to which units are represented by the balance on the account. The job cost subsidiary shows which units are under construction and which cost categories have been processed through the system.

Again, critical to the integrity of the system is to have the total of all units in the job cost subsidiary equal the balance in the general ledger in the work in process account. A discrepancy between the general ledger and the subsidiary is indicative that errors were made when entering and processing the transactions into the system. At this point, the accuracy of the numbers is questionable and managers will be reluctant to base decisions on information that cannot be validated.

The use of computers for data processing does not guarantee equality between subsidiary and general ledgers. Even though some systems have safeguards to help the data entry clerk maintain the equality between the two systems, other software programs have no safeguards and so it is up to the accountant to set up processes and procedures to verify the equality between the control account and the subsidiary on a continuous basis.

Once management loses confidence in the credibility of the accounting information, it is very hard to gain

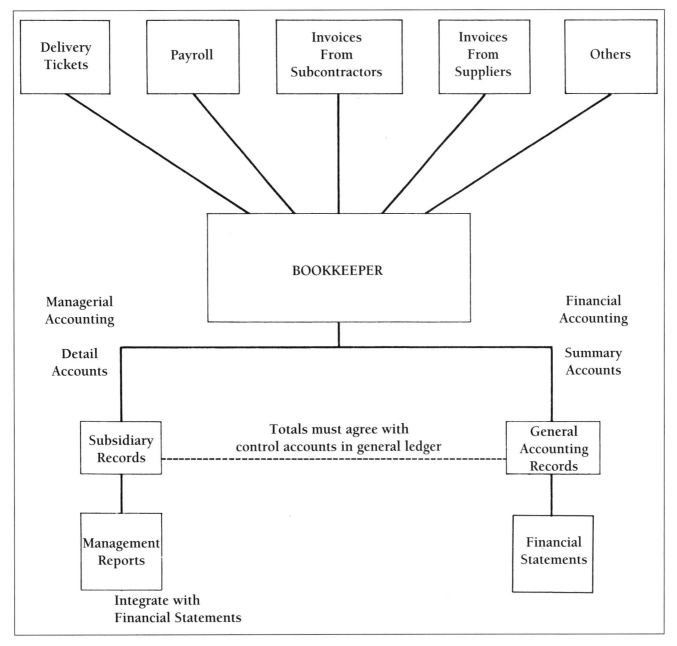

Figure 2–2. Flow of data through the system.

back their confidence. Managers need to trust the financial information generated by the system if they are going to use the system as a management tool.

The general ledger entry indicates that the builder bought merchandise on credit for use in the construction of a house; the accounts payable subsidiary shows how much they owed XYZ Lumber Company; and the job cost subsidiary shows the cost of lumber used in house number 15. Remember that the total

of all individual accounts in a subsidiary must agree with the balance in the general ledger account.

A remodeler or developer follows the same procedure for materials he or she purchases. Instead of using the work in process account, the remodeler uses the direct cost of remodeling account. The subsidiary ledger identifies the job for which the materials were used by a number assigned at the start of each job. The developer uses the cost of land

Example 2-1: A home builder purchased materials on account from XYZ Lumber Company to be used in house number 15. The builder records the financial information in the following places:

- The general ledger, under work in process and accounts payable
- The accounts payable subsidiary, under

- the XYZ Lumber Company account
- The job cost subsidiary, under job number 15

and development account and identifies the specific subdivision by a given number.

Accounting Equation

The general accounting system rests on a single algebraic equation:

$$Assets = Equities$$

where assets represents things of value owned by the company such as cash, inventories, furniture, and equipment, and equities represents the source of capital from the owners, creditors, or lenders to acquire the assets. Thus, we can expand the equity side of the equation to say:

$$Equities = Liabilities\ (Debt) + Owner's\ Equity\ (Investment)$$

Accounting is often referred to as a double entry system. A double entry system requires that every financial transaction be recorded in at least two different accounts. For example, a person decides to open a homebuilding business. After the appropriate business structure (sole proprietorship, partnership, or corporation) is set up, the owner goes to the bank to open a business account with $20,000.

The accounting entry to record this transaction requires that cash be recorded in the cash account or asset side of the equation and that the investment be recorded in the equity side:

$$Assets = Equities$$
$$Cash\ \$20,000 = Owner's\ Equity\ \$20,000$$

The accounting equation follows the same principles of any other algebraic equation; the left side of the equation must always equal the right side of the equation. It is through the double entry concept that the equality of the equation is always maintained.

Now let's look into the components of the equation in more detail:

Assets

Assets represent all things of value owned by the business, including tangible goods and future benefits. Examples of assets are cash; accounts receivables; inventories such as materials, land, work in process, finished units; office furniture and equipment; construction equipment and vehicles; and prepaid expenses.

Some assets are intangible in nature and represent future benefits and/or rights. For example, accounts receivables represent the right to collect cash sometime in the future and prepaid expenses represent the right to receive a service in the future. Most of the assets for a typical homebuilding and land development company are inventories, either land to be or in the process of being developed or houses under construction. Remodelers, conversely, do not have much in the way of inventories except for some construction materials because typically they do not own the properties they work on.

Equities

Equities represent claims to the assets of a business by creditors, lenders, owners, and investors. The claims of creditors and lenders are generally referred to as liabilities and include accounts such as accounts payable, notes payable, and construction loans payable. The claims of owners are referred to as owners' equity. Owners' equity consists of two basic elements: the owners' investment and the accumulation of net income or losses from operating the business. The owners bear the risk of operating the business, thus increasing their portion of the equity if the business makes a profit or reducing their equity if the business loses money.

Let's go back to the asset equation. Through the operation of the business the assets of the company now equal $700,000, thus the equation will look like this:

$$\text{Assets} = \text{Equities}$$
$$\$700,000 = \$700,000$$

If we now break down the equities into third parties and owners, the equity side of the equation looks like this:

$$\text{Equities} = \text{Liabilities} + \text{Owners' Equity}$$
$$\$700,000 = \$500,000 + \$200,000$$

Putting both parts together the equation looks like this:

$$\text{Assets} = \text{Liabilities} + \text{Owners' Equity}$$
$$\$700,000 = \$500,000 + \$200,000$$

Remember that the owners' equity section represents not only the initial investment but also the accumulated net income or profits from the start of operations. However, any cash withdrawals or distributions by the owners will decrease the accumulated net income.

Chapter 7 discusses the elements of this equation in greater detail.

Debits and Credits

The terms *debit* and *credit* are meaningless unless they are used in conjunction with the general accounting classifications of assets, liabilities, and owners' equity. By convention, debit balances represent assets and credit balances represent liabilities and owners' equity.

$$\text{Assets} = \text{Liabilities} + \text{Owners' Equity}$$
$$\text{Dr} = \text{Cr} + \text{Cr}$$

Traditionally, understanding debits and credits has been the nightmare of many accounting students. To understand how debits and credits work, let's go back to basic mathematical principles of adding like signs and subtracting unlike signs. For example, under mathematical principles we always add two or more positive numbers as well as two or more negative numbers; in both instances we are dealing with liked signs. When we have a negative number and a positive number we subtract one number from the other and the sign of the higher number prevails. The same is true when working with debits and credits.

When looking at the accounting equation, the two credits on the right side of the equation are added, thus validating the equation.

$$\$700,000 = \$500,000 + \$200,000$$
$$\$700,000 = \$700,000$$

When financial transactions are recorded, the first step is to determine the traditional balance of the accounts affected by the transaction; the second step is to determine if the transaction increases or decreases the accounts. For example, take the initial entry we made when starting operations. A business account was set up at the bank in the amount of $20,000. The cash deposit increased the assets of the company. Cash is recognized as an asset that is represented by debit balances; thus, to increase the cash account from $0 to $20,000, we need to debit the account. The complementary side of this transaction is the source of the cash; it came from the owner, which means an increase in owners' equity from $0 to $20,000. Owners' equity is represented by a credit balance, thus to increase the owners' equity we need to credit the owners' equity account. The transaction will look like this:

Debit cash (asset) for $20,000

Credit capital contribution (owners' equity) for $20,000

Using the accounting equation format:

$$Assets = Liabilities + Owners'\ Equity$$
$$\$20,000 = 0 + \$20,000$$

Thus, we can draw the following generalities:

- To increase assets that are generally represented by debit balances (Dr), debit the assets: Dr + Dr.
- To increase liabilities that are generally represented by credit balances (Cr), credit the liability: Cr + Cr.

- To increase owners' equity that is generally represented by credit balances (Cr), credit the owners' equity: Cr + Cr.
- To decrease assets that are generally represented by debit balances (Dr), credit the assets: Dr − Cr.
- To decrease liabilities that are generally represented by credit balances (Cr), debit the liability: Cr − Dr.
- To decrease owners' equity that is generally represented by credit balances (Cr), debit the owners' equity: Cr − Dr.

Let's take a look at some examples on how to record typical financial transactions:

EXAMPLE 2-2

The company buys two computers and a printer for the office and pays $1,000 in cash and signs a note to pay the balance of $3,000 in $250/month installments. Analyzing the transaction the results are as follows:

1. The company acquires an asset (office equipment) valued at $4,000, thus increasing the total assets.
2. The company used $1,000 cash, also an asset, to acquire the equipment, thus the assets (cash) were reduced by $1,000.
3. The company signs a note payable promising to pay a creditor the balance of $3,000 in $250/ month installments, thus increasing the liabilities.

Placing these steps in the accounting equation, it looks like this:

Assets = Liabilities + Owners' Equity
1. Dr $4,000
2. Cr ($1,000)
3. Cr $3,000
   $3,000 = $3,000

The company pays the first $250 installment:

1. Cash, an asset, is reduced by $250.
2. Notes payable, a liability, is reduced by $250.

Assets = Liabilities + Owners' Equity
1. Cr ($250)
2. Dr ($250)
   $250 = $250

EXAMPLE 2-3

The company puts down a deposit on a lot. The required deposit is $5,000. The total cost of the lot is $35,000. The balance is due at closing.

1. The company commits a deposit of $5,000 for future rights to buy a lot, thus increasing its assets.
2. The company pays $5,000 in cash for the right to purchase a lot, thus decreasing an asset.

Assets = Liabilities + Owners' Equity
1. Dr $5,000
2. Cr ($5,000)
   0 = 0

The company closes on the lot and takes ownership. The balance on the lot is paid through a loan.

1. The company acquires an asset, the lot, thus increasing its assets by $35,000.
2. The company uses the $5,000 deposit (an asset) as part payment on the lot, thus decreasing the assets.
3. The company takes out a loan for $30,000, a liability, to finance the balance on the lot.

Assets = Liabilities + Owners' Equity
1. Dr $35,000
2. Cr ($5,000)
3. Cr $30,000
   $30,000 = $30,000

EXAMPLE 2-4

A developer purchases a small parcel of undeveloped land for $750,000 according to the following terms: $100,000 in cash with a mortgage of $650,000 payable in full in 5 years, with interest at 10 percent payable quarterly. When the contract is closed, the following accounts are affected:

1. Cash, an asset, decreases by $100,000.
2. Land, an asset, increases by $750,000.
3. Notes payable, a liability, increases by $650,000.

Placing the transaction under the accounting equation helps to verify that the equation balances:

Assets = Liabilities + Owners' Equity
1. Cr ($100,000)
2. Dr $750,000
3. Cr $650,000
   $650,000 = $650,000

EXAMPLE 2-5

A builder sells a house for $125,000 and pays a sales commission of 6 percent. The seller pays various closing costs for the buyer that amount to $1,150. The cost of the house includes land costs of $22,000 and construction costs of $75,450. Loans on the property amount to $86,500. Analyzing the transaction the results are as follows:

1. Revenues are realized; owners' equity increases by $125,000.
2. The builder incurs expenses associated with the sale; owners' equity is reduced by $6,500 (sales commission) and $1,150 (closing costs).
3. The builder repays the loan; loans payable, a liability, is reduced by $86,500.

4. The builder receives cash; cash, an asset, increases by $30,850.
5. Costs are associated with the sale; owners' equity is reduced by $97,450 (land, $22,000; construction costs, $75,450).
6. Inventories are reduced; land, an asset is reduced by $22,000, and work in process (construction cost), an asset, is reduced by $75,450.

Assets = Liabilities + Owners' Equity
1. Cr $125,000
2. Dr $6,500 + $1,150
3. Dr $86,500
4. Dr $30,850
5. Dr $22,000 + $75,450
6. Cr $22,000 + $75,450
   ($66,600) = ($86,500) + $19,900
   ($66,600) = ($66,600)

Stores and financial institutions often confuse our understanding of debits and credits. Banks and stores use debits and credits to reflect what happens to their accounting records when a client or customer makes a transaction rather than to show how the transaction affects the client's records. For example, when someone opens a checking account at a bank and makes a deposit, a claim is created on the assets of the bank. In other words, the client has the right to withdraw the funds at any time. The bank is merely holding the funds owned by the client. The bank's accounting records show the claim as a liability or credit because it represents an obligation on the part of the bank to return the cash to the account holder on demand. With every new deposit, the claim increases and the bank credits the client's account to show the increase in the bank's liability. Conversely, when the client takes money out of the account, the claim is satisfied, the liability is decreased, and the account is thus debited.

Translating such a transaction to a company's accounting records can be confusing. The transaction will be the reverse of the one recorded in the bank's accounting system. When a company makes a deposit to a bank account, the cash balance on the account increases and creates a debit to the cash account in the company's records. Conversely, a withdrawal decreases the asset and requires a credit to the cash account.

Net Income

Net income or net loss is what is left over from the sale after all costs and expenses are accounted for. To compute net income, subtract from sales the cost of sales (cost of the lots and direct construction costs on the houses sold) and all expenses necessary to run the business. As stated earlier, the owners' equity accumulates all the results of operations from prior years. Revenues or sales increase the owners' equity, and, conversely, cost of sales and operating expenses decrease the owners' equity.

$$\text{Net Income} = \text{Revenues} - \text{Cost of Sales} - \text{Operating Expenses}$$

Add this dimension to the accounting equation:

$$\text{Assets} = \text{Liabilities} + \text{Owners' Equity}$$
$$\text{Dr} = \text{Cr} = \text{Cr}$$
$$\text{Revenues} = \text{Cost of Sales} - \text{Operating Expense}$$
$$\text{Cr} = \text{Dr} - \text{Dr}$$

Revenues

Revenues represent the consideration earned from providing goods and services to third parties. All profit-oriented organizations are in business to generate revenues. For the home builder or remodeler, sales of houses or remodeling jobs are the most important source of revenues. For developers it will be the sale of developed tracts of land or finished lots. Credit balances represent revenues because revenues increase the owners' equity.

Cost of Sales

The term *cost* has a double connotation that distinctly separates it from the term *expense*. Cost is associated with the creation of value and therefore is considered an asset, a thing of value owned by the business prior to the sale. Take as an example the building of a house, the cost of materials, and the labor used in the process. As construction progresses, the cost of materials and labor adds value to the house, thus increasing the value of the asset, in this case work in process inventory. Why, then, is cost of sales considered a reduction of owners' equity? When a house is sold, the company no longer has the right to the asset. The sale generates revenues, but it also creates the loss of an asset hopefully of a lesser value than the revenues. The cost of the house reduces the amount of revenue received on the transaction and thus decreases the owners' equity.

Builders, remodelers, and developers deal with two types of construction costs: direct and indirect.

Direct Construction Cost

Direct construction costs are easily identified because they can be traced to a specific unit of production. Examples include the cost of materials such as asphalt for roads (for developers), lumber, bricks, paint, and kitchen appliances (for builders and remodelers) and the cost of labor hours of workers such as excavators, framers, roofers, and masons. These costs contribute to the creation of value; therefore, they increase the value of the work in process inventories.

Indirect Construction Costs

Indirect construction costs do not relate to a particular unit of production but to the construction process itself. Examples of indirect construction costs include salaries of field supervisory personnel, field offices, field vehicles, temporary utilities, storage facilities, Nextel phones, and any other expense necessary to carry out the construction process. Because these costs are necessary to the construction process and contribute to the creation of value, builders, remodelers, and developers should add them to the work in process. In other words, they are part of the cost of building a house, completing a remodeling job, or developing a tract of land.

Builders, remodelers, and developers commonly use the terms *overhead* and *soft costs* for indirect construction costs. These terms generally include indirect construction costs plus some or all other operating expenses. Whenever overhead cost or soft cost is used, be sure you understand the type of costs and expenses to which it refers. In future chapters we will expand on how to account for these costs and how to go about allocating them to cost of sales and work in process.

Operating Expenses

Operating expenses are necessary expenditures incurred during the operation of a business. They are generally associated with a given period of time—a month, a quarter, or a year—rather than with a unit of production; therefore, they are commonly referred to as period costs. In accounting, operating expenses for a given period are subtracted from revenues received during the same period of time. Operating expenses are further classified into financing, sales and marketing, and general and administrative expenses. Expenses relate to the passage of time, not to the units of production.

Financing Expenses

Financing expenses represent the cost of borrowing money from financial institutions or other third-party sources. These expenses traditionally are associated with the passage of time on a loan. However, financing expenses often can be traced directly to a specific house or project.

Under certain circumstances, tax legislation requires that builders, remodelers, and developers consider financing expenses directly related to units of production as costs and, therefore, they must be inventoried. To assure legal compliance, builders, remodelers, and developers should discuss regulations pertaining to the classification of financing expenses with the company's accountant or tax consultant each year. Even though for management purposes it is recommended that the interest accounts be set up as an operating expense, builders, remodelers, and developers need to be able to retrieve the information to make the necessary adjustments for tax purposes.

Sales and Marketing Expenses

Sales and marketing expenses are incurred to support the sales and marketing effort. They are associated with a given period of time and are charged off to the revenues received during the same period. In certain instances builders must capitalize the start-up marketing expenses of a new project. Start-up marketing expenses for small-volume builders usually are not significant enough to capitalize.

General and Administrative Expenses

General and administrative expenses are all other expenses (other than financing and sales and marketing) necessary to operate a business. These expenses can include office supplies, telephone service, administrative salaries, office rent, books and subscriptions, and insurance. They are associated with a specific period of time and are charged off against revenues received during the same period.

Figure 2–3 shows the flow of costs through the various accounts in the system from the time the cost is incurred to the closing of the sale. To summarize the concepts presented in this chapter, assets represent items of value owned by the business and equities establish who has the claims to the assets, either creditors or owners. Revenues, cost, and operating expenses measure profits or losses, and, in turn, profits and losses impact the owners' share of the assets.

Financial Statements

The two most commonly used financial statements produced by the accounting system are the income statement (also know as profit and loss statement) and the balance sheet.

Income Statement

The income statement summarizes the operation of the company for a given period of time, be it a month, several months, or a year. All sources of revenue are presented in the income statement together with all costs associated with the revenues and the operating expenses for the reporting period of time. The result is the net income or net loss produced by the company during the reporting period.

**Net Income =
Revenues − Cost of Sales − Operating Expense**

The income statement is a dynamic statement because it summarizes the economic activity during a set period of time—1 month, one quarter, 6 months,

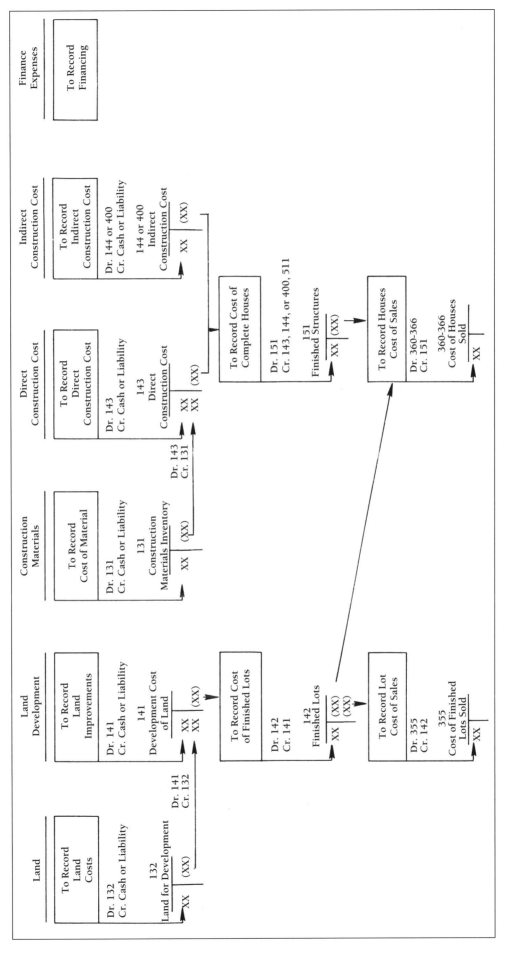

Figure 2–3. Flow of costs through the system.

or 1 year, but normally for a period no longer than 1 year.

The format used in preparing the income statement will have an impact on how much information you can obtain from the statement. There are three main sections in any income statement: the revenues, the cost of sales, and the operating expenses. It is not unusual to see the operating expenses on an income statement listed in alphabetical order. This format makes it difficult to analyze how well each functional area performed during the period.

In contrast, if the expenses are accumulated by functional areas—construction, financing, sales and marketing, general and administrative—with a subtotal after each category, you can easily see how much each functional area costs to operate. A quick evaluation can be made as to the efficiency of each function.

The following example of an income statement shows the format using the totals for each functional area.

XYZ Home Building Company
Income Statement
For year ended 20XX

Revenue:	
Sales—Single Family	$29,650,000
Cost of Sales:	
Land	$3,700,000
Direct Cost	$17,150,000
Total Cost of Sales	$20,850,000
Gross Profit	**$8,800,000**
Operating Expenses:	
Indirect Construction Costs	$860,000
Financing Expenses	$1,560,000
Sales & Marketing	$2,200,000
General & Administrative	$1,425,000
Total Operating Expenses	$6,045,000
Net Operating Income	**$2,755,000**

Balance Sheet

In contrast to the income statement, the balance sheet is a static statement that represents the financial position of a business as of the date of the balance sheet. It shows how many and what types of assets the business owns and who has claims to the assets. It represents the accounting equation on a financial statement format.

Assets = Liabilities + Owners' Equity

XYZ Home Building Company
Balance Sheet
December 31, 20xx

ASSETS
Current Assets:
Cash	$985,000
Inventories—Land	$10,200,000
Inventories—Work in Process	$4,500,000
Total Current Assets	$15,685,000
Other Assets	$1,450,000
Total Assets	**$17,135,000**

LIABILITIES & OWNERS' EQUITY
Liabilities:
Current Liabilities	$9,200,000
Long-term Liabilities	$4,300,000
Total Liabilities	$13,500,000
Owners' Equity	$3,635,000
Total Liabilities & Owners' Equity	**$17,135,000**

Chapter 7 includes a detailed discussion of the income statement and balance sheet. Although the financial statements present information in general classifications, builders, remodelers, and developers find them valuable to the decision-making process and the control of the business by comparing current results with prior years and industry performance, applying trend and ratio analysis and other analytical tools. Chapter 8 discusses financial analysis techniques and how to use them to improve business operations and profitability.

Users of Financial Information

Owners and Managers

Owners and managers of building, remodeling, and development businesses should be the primary users of the financial information generated by the accounting system. The information generated by the system allows managers to monitor the financial results on an on-going basis. It also lets owners moni-tor the return on their investment and the general health of the company. The owners are responsible for setting general goals and direction for their companies. In carrying out this function, they find the ratios and trends computed from the financial statements of great value (see Chapter 8).

Managers are responsible for carrying out the goals and following the direction set by the owners. In fulfilling this function, managers monitor the day-to-day operations of the company. They use financial statements and management reports generated from a well-designed accounting system to measure performance and make comparisons with budgets in a timely manner. Thus, financial reports provide managers with a tool to evaluate the profitability of the operations. The types of reports and degree of detail required by each manager depend on, among other things, the scope of the manager's responsibility. The broader the scope, the more general or condensed the manager's reports. The closer the manager is to the actual operations, the more detailed the reports need to be.

Lenders

The lenders use the financial information to determine the ability of builders, remodelers, and developers to repay loans. Lenders look for a measure of liquidity and profitability that will somehow ensure that the borrower will continue in business and have the resources to repay the loan. Lenders are concerned almost exclusively with the traditional financial statements. In many instances they require some type of certification of or opinion about the financial statements from an independent certified public accountant (CPA).

Investors

Investors used the traditional financial statements to forecast potential profitability of an investment. Analysis of the traditional statements can disclose a level of profitability, leverage factor, liquidity, holding power, and risk factor. Analyzing trends by comparing financial information for a number of years can provide potential investors with a good measurement of a company's profitability.

Reporting Requirements

Reporting requirements vary significantly from company to company depending on the size of the operation and the number of employees. At the very least, companies of all sizes should prepare financial statements on a monthly basis. The use of computers has allowed companies to produce an over-abundance of very detailed reports. As a result, the reporting system has a tendency to turn into a data dump instead of supplying meaningful information. Producing and reviewing unnecessary reports wastes time and loses focus from the main issues. To determine the value of a report, ask if the report will guide action. If not, the report probably is unnecessary and can be eliminated.

The more employees a company has, the more reports the company will need as the owner or managers become more and more removed from the front line. To keep control and monitor and direct the overall profitability of the company, top managers need reports measuring performance of line managers in accordance with predetermined goals. Line managers (those directing the actual construction, remodeling, or development process) need reports with cost codes that measure the details of the different construction phases and how they compare with predetermined or estimated costs.

Audit Trail

The Internal Revenue Service requires adequate record-keeping to be able to verify the validity of the company's tax returns. Reviews and audits also require an audit trail. This trail provides the ability to trace any financial transaction to its originating document (for instance, for accounts payable, the ability to trace a transaction to the original invoice).

In a medium- to large-size building company in which authority is delegated to a number of employees, conducting an annual audit is wise. As the owner delegates authority, the owner begins to lose direct control over some of the accounting functions. An annual audit verifies that the accounting function is being carried out according to generally accepted accounting principles (GAAP), and it could also disclose fraud. An internal system of checks and balances should be in place to decrease the possibility of fraud. Some of these checks and balances require the segregation of functions such as record-keeping, custodianship of assets (who physically has possession and control of the assets), authorization for use of assets, and operations. For example, whenever possible, the functions of purchasing, accounting, check writing, and check signing should be carried out by different employees. In a small-volume firm where one individual might be responsible for more than one of these functions, the owner should maintain control of at least the check-signing function.

CHAPTER 3

Accounting Methods and Terms

Accounting Methods

Builders, remodelers, and developers use a number of methods to maintain accounting records and keep track of revenues, costs, and expenses. The method you choose to process data does not alter the effectiveness of the system as a whole; however, procedures and output may vary slightly. This chapter provides an overview of some of these methods and discusses accounting practices and terminology common to the homebuilding industry.

Accounting serves many purposes. It especially provides a way to determine net income or profits for a given period. When you are computing profit, the primary concern is to determine which costs and expenses relate to which revenues. The builder has several alternatives for recording revenues, costs, and expenses, including:

- Cash or accrual—timing for entering transactions in the system
- Completed contract or percentage of completion—procedure for recognizing revenues
- Direct costing or absorption costing—procedure for allocating construction costs to units of production

Cash or Accrual

Builders, developers, and remodelers may use either the cash method or the accrual method for recording the financial transactions into the accounting system. The accrual method generally provides more timely and accurate information. The cash method, conversely, is less complicated and therefore easier to use. It can be effective for a small-volume company if the owner is a hands-on manager.

Cash

A cash accounting system reports revenues, costs, and expenses in the accounting period in which cash is received or disbursed, regardless of when the revenues are earned or the expenses are incurred. The bookkeeper records only the cash transactions, that is, the cash deposits made on a given day and the checks written on the same day. Because of the lag between recognition of revenues and actual receipt of cash and the delay between commitment to cost or expenses and the actual cash disbursement, financial statements and management reports do not reflect current financial conditions. However, a cash system is the easiest way to keep financial records because you record only cash exchanges.

Accrual

An accrual accounting system records revenues and expenses when they are earned and incurred, regardless of when the cash transaction takes place. Therefore, the accrual system presents a more up-to-date picture of a company's financial condition. When an invoice is received and approved for payment, the bookkeeper enters it immediately into the system, even though payment will not take place until later. Under this system, job cost reports are more current because costs are entered into the system when an invoice is received rather than when it is paid.

For example, the invoice for a purchase of material made on January 27—after the supplier's billing is closed for the month—would not be included in the supplier's statement to the customer until February.

Payment would not be due until March 31, 2 months after the cost was incurred. Under the cash method, the invoice would be entered in the accounting system when the check is written—as late as March 31. Under the accrual method, the bookkeeper records the purchase when he or she receives the invoice with the verification from the field that the materials have been received as ordered and in good condition.

Under the accrual method, cash received but not earned is recognized as a liability rather than as income. In the cash system, cash is recognized as income when received. Generally, a contract to sell a home or lot requires a deposit. Contracts are sometimes canceled before closing and deposits returned. Under the cash system, the deposits will already be counted as revenues; therefore, revenues must be reduced when the deposit is reimbursed. In a remodeling company, deposits are also made on contracts. However, the work is generally done on the client's property and even if a contract is canceled the remodeler probably has earned the amount of the deposit for the work done prior to the cancellation.

A common misconception of the accrual system is that it hinders the control of cash because revenues and expenses do not measure cash inflows and outflows. However, cash is controlled by recording all cash inflows and outflows in the cash account.

Lenders and potential investors favor the use of the accrual system because it presents a more up-to-date picture of a company's financial condition. It also makes a builder, remodeler, or developer look more sophisticated, which, in turn, increases the company's credibility and the level of comfort lenders and potential investors have with the company. The accrual system clearly matches revenues and expenses more accurately than the cash system and presents a timelier picture of the company's financial condition.

Completed Contract or Percentage of Completion

Builders and developers often face the problem of spreading income over the life of a construction job that extends over several fiscal or calendar-year periods.

Both the completed contract and the percentage of completion methods are accepted accounting procedures for recognizing revenues. However, percentage of completion can only be used for jobs that are sold or built under enforceable contracts and are in process at the end of the accounting period. The method selected directly affects the company's taxable income for a given year. Therefore, tax regulations might determine which method you are required to use. The appropriate method to use depends on the average dollar volume of revenues for the past 3 years and the nature of the construction activity. Because tax regulations are subject to change from year to year, make sure you comply with the current version. The cost for speculative jobs must accrue in an inventory account, and no revenues can be recognized until the transaction is completed and settled.

Completed Contract

Home builders (especially production and custom builders), remodelers, and developers probably use this method most frequently for recognition of income and cost of sales. It does not recognize revenues and cost of sales until work is completed and the sales contract has been fully executed. The bookkeeper records all costs related to the contract in an inventory account, and enters cash received for the job—advance payments or contract deposits—into a liability, or deferred revenue, account. At the completion of the job, the bookkeeper transfers the costs to a cost of sales account and the contract deposits to a revenue account. Under this method, the recognition of revenues and cost of sales is postponed until the sale is closed. The recognition of any profits on the sale is also postponed until the date of closing. Obviously for tax purposes this is a more favorable method to use, and under present tax regulations, home builders can always report sales using the completed contract method, regardless of sales volume. Because tax regulations are always subject to change, you need to check the regulations in effect at the end of each taxable year.

Percentage of Completion

This method recognizes revenues and cost of sales as the job progresses. You can use it only on jobs that are

being built under contract. A custom home builder, remodeler, or a light industrial general contractor might choose to use this method.

To determine revenues earned at the end of the accounting period, calculate the percentage of completion for each job based on costs to date as a percentage of total job costs and apply it to the total value of the contract. Apply the same percentage of related cost to cost of sales. Thus, if a job extends over several years and construction is 40 percent complete at the end of an accounting period, you would recognize 40 percent of estimated revenues and 40 percent of estimated cost for that period.

A word of caution: Calculating the percent of completion can be tricky for some jobs. The amount recognized as revenue is no more accurate than an estimate would be. Be careful with your calculations when determining the percent completed, otherwise, the resulting reports can be misleading and falsely represent a company's financial status.

Direct Costing or Absorption Costing

Costing is the process of allocating construction costs to units of production such as finished lots, houses, or remodeled jobs. Direct costing and absorption costing are methods of accumulating cost. As discussed in Chapter 2, costs are classified as either direct or indirect.

Even though direct costing is used as an analytical tool in managerial accounting, the American Institute of Certified Public Accountants (AICPA) and the Internal Revenue Service recognize absorption costing as the accepted method for product costing.

Direct Costing

Under the direct costing method, only direct costs are inventoried. Indirect costs are considered period costs and are charged off to revenues in the period in which they are incurred. This method facilitates analysis of each cost and expense component.

Absorption Costing

When using absorption costing both direct and indirect costs are inventoried. Inventories show a greater dollar value under this method; therefore, net income is higher.

Let's take a look at an example using both methods and comparing the results under each methodology. During the month of January, three houses are built at a direct cost of $80,000 each, including cost of land. The total indirect cost is $15,000, or $5,000 per unit. Two houses are sold for $110,000 each; one house remains in inventory. Operating expenses for the month amount to $20,000.

	Direct Costing	Absorption Costing
Inventory Valuation:		
Direct Cost	$80,000	$80,000
Indirect Cost		$5,000
Total	**$80,000**	**$85,000**
Computation of Cost of Sales:		
Direct Cost (2 houses)	$160,000	$160,000
Indirect Cost		$10,000
Total	**$160,000**	**$170,000**
Computation of Net Income—January		
Sales	$220,000	$220,000
Cost of Sales	$160,000	$170,000
Gross Profit	**$60,000**	**$50,000**
Indirect Cost	$15,000	
Operating Expenses	$20,000	$20,000
Net Income	**$25,000**	**$30,000**
House Closed in February		
Sales	$110,000	$110,000
Cost of Sales	$80,000	$85,000
Gross Profit	**$30,000**	**$25,000**
TOTAL Net Income	**$55,000**	**$55,000**

After all three houses are closed, the net income from the three houses will be the same under both methods. There will be a timing difference in the recognition of net income, but the amount of net income ultimately will be the same.

Terms

A number of accounting terms are often misused or misunderstood. This section defines and explains what they truly mean and their significance within the accounting system.

Revenues Versus Cash Receipts

Revenues and cash have different meanings in accounting, regardless of whether a cash or an accrual system is used. Cash receipts do not come only from revenue sources. Cash receipts can come from collections on accounts receivables, proceeds from the sale of a fixed asset (i.e., furniture and equipment), refunds on returned merchandise, capital contributions from owners, and loans.

Expenses Versus Cash Disbursements

By the same token, not all cash disbursements are expenses or costs. Cash disbursements may represent investments in land, equipment, securities, payments on loans, dividends, or payments on accounts payable. Furthermore, some expenses that do not require a cash disbursement—such as depreciation—must be recognized under either a cash or an accrual system as an expense.

Profit Versus Cash Balance

Because all cash receipts are not considered revenues and all cash disbursements are not expenses, a company's cash balance does not equal profits. Profits and cash are separate measurements of basic elements in a company's finances—revenues and expenses for profits, and cash sources and disbursements for cash balance. Under no circumstances is one a measure of the other.

Expenses Versus Cost

The terms *expense* and *cost* should not be used interchangeably because the two terms have distinct meanings. Cost is associated with a manufacturing process and is considered a business asset until the manufactured product—such as a new house—is sold. Costs are accumulated in an inventory account that represents the value of the structures under construction. Expenses, conversely, are associated with the day-to-day operation of a business. They are sometimes referred to as period costs because they are charged off against revenues received during the same period of time in which the expenses are incurred. Examples include financing, sales and marketing, and administrative expenses.

Indirect Construction Cost Versus Overhead

Indirect construction costs, sometimes also referred to as "soft costs," are the costs associated with the building process. They cannot be directly traced to a particular unit of production, only to the process.

Overhead is somewhat synonymous with indirect construction costs, but in many instances it could also include sales expenses, financing expenses, and a portion of the general and administrative expenses. Because overhead can include indirect costs and one or more types of expenses, you should always clarify what is included when the term is used.

Fixed Versus Variable Cost or Expense

Cost and expenses can be fixed or variable. Fixed cost and expenses will remain constant within a volume range. In other words, fixed cost will remain the same regardless of the number of houses built within a volume range. The more units produced within the range, the lower the cost per unit; conversely, the lower the number of units, the higher the cost per unit.

These types of cost and expenses are generally controlled by top management, as typically they relate to changes in personnel, leases on space and equipment, and office costs. Office rent, telephones, and salaries are examples of fixed expenses. On a per-unit basis, fixed cost and expenses will change as the number of units, jobs, or lots built changes.

In contrast, variable cost and expenses increase or decrease proportionately with increases or decreases in the units of production. In other words, variable cost and expenses relate directly to the number of units built. The more units built, the higher the variable costs or expenses. For example, the cost for lumber will increase proportionately to the number of houses built. By the same token, as production decreases, so do the variable cost and expenses. On a per-unit basis, variable costs remain constant.

It is essential to understand the differences between fixed and variable cost and expenses because the control procedures for each type are different. Generally, variable cost and expenses are controllable at a lower management level than are fixed cost and expenses. In the construction process the superintendent can generally control variable cost, while the project manager, production manager, or a higher level of management will have control over fixed cost. Efficiency and productivity are key concepts in the control of fixed cost and expenses on a per-unit basis because production levels have a significant impact on the per-unit cost.

CHAPTER 4

Chart of Accounts

Structure

A list of accounts, commonly referred to as a chart of accounts, serves as the structure of the accounting system. Each account is a center for accumulating data. These accounts determine how much detail the system will generate, what type of information the system will report, and how much control a builder, remodeler, or developer will be able to exercise through the financial information. Because the chart of accounts is the foundation of any firm's accounting system, the company's owners and accountant should be involved in carefully designing the system to ensure that it will meet the company's specific reporting requirements and provide the structure for the control systems.

As discussed in Chapter 2, an accounting system has two levels: the financial or general ledger and the managerial or subsidiary ledgers. The chart of accounts must accurately reflect these two levels. At the financial level, the accounting system accumulates data in a summary format and generates reports such as the balance sheet and the income statement. The subsidiary ledgers break down and accumulate the data in a detailed format for management analysis, reporting, and control. The subsidiary ledgers generate job cost reports for each construction unit, job, or lot; status reports on construction loans; gross profit analysis on units sold; and other reports.

In designing a chart of accounts you should follow a number of guidelines. The chart must include the five general accounting classifications, and accounts should be grouped under the respective classifications: assets, liabilities and owners' equity, revenues, and expenses. It must allow for the classification of data in sufficient detail to satisfy fiscal requirements and management needs. Expenses should be further classified under each functional area to facilitate analysis of the financial information generated by the system. Functional areas include indirect construction costs or construction expenses, financing expenses, sales and marketing expenses, and general and administrative expenses.

The chart of accounts should be uniform and consistent to ensure comparability with previous fiscal periods, plans, and budgets. Furthermore, the estimating, purchasing, and scheduling systems should be integrated with the accounting system with the objective of having a seamless system that facilitates coordination and increases efficiency in each department and at every level of operation. The chart of accounts must also be flexible enough to allow for future changes with a minimal amount of disruption to the system as a whole, and it must have the capacity to expand to meet new financial and management requirements.

Numerical Coding System

A numerical coding system, usually used with the chart of accounts, provides a convenient method of identifying each account. A well-designed coding system assures uniformity and standardization within the system, allows for flexibility, and facilitates conversion from a manual accounting system to a computerized system.

The numerical coding in a chart of accounts must follow a logical sequence to help identify each account's general category and subcategory. A coding structure of four digits is satisfactory for small- to medium-size builders, developers, and remodelers.

Large-volume builders and developers might need as many as eight-digit codes to accommodate additional account detail and classifications. Expanding businesses can expand their coding structure by adding one or two digits to the existing four-digit coding. However, a chart of accounts must be as simple as possible and digits should be added only when necessary. The charts of accounts contained in Appendixes A through D are approved by NAHB and ensure uniformity and comparability of financial information within the building, land development, and remodeling industries.

The general accounting categories and their recommended numerical coding are as follows:

1000	Assets
2000	Liabilities and owners' equity
3000	Sales, revenues, and cost of sales
4000	Indirect construction cost or construction expenses
5000	Financing expenses
6000	Sales and marketing expenses
7000	Rental properties expenses
8000	General and administrative expenses
9000	Other revenues and other expenses

The second digit in the numerical coding system generally identifies a subclassification within a general classification. For example:

1000–1999	Assets
1000	Cash
1100	Short-term investments
1200	Receivables
1400	Inventories

The third digit provides a further breakdown of each subclassification:

1000	Cash
1010	Petty cash
1020	Cash on deposit, general
1030	Cash on deposit, payroll
1040	Cash on deposit, savings

The fourth digit can provide further breakdown as follows:

1020 Cash on deposit, general
1021 Cash—First National Bank
1022 Cash—Second National Bank
1023 Cash—Great Northern Bank
1024 Cash—First Savings and Loan

Customizing the Chart of Accounts

Appendix A provides an outline of the chart of accounts discussed in this chapter. This chart of accounts has been revised and expanded to include special accounts used by remodelers, developers, and multiproject and commercial builders. Appendix B presents a detailed breakdown of the chart of accounts. It provides descriptions of each account, including the type of data that you should accumulate in the account, and explains the specific requirements for using the account. Appendix B also tells which accounts should be used exclusively to record financial data generated by development, remodeling, and multiproject and commercial building activities. Appendix C outlines basic accounts for small-volume builders, remodelers, and developers. Most small-volume builders, remodelers, and developers use the major account classifications in this chart. However, some might not use all of the accounts presented and others might need to add accounts. In other words, you need to customize the chart of accounts presented here to reflect the structure of your company and the way it does business. Customizing the chart should be simple because the chart presented here has been designed with flexibility for addition or deletion of accounts.

CHAPTER 5

Bookkeeping Procedures

As discussed earlier, an accounting system consists of two tracks that operate simultaneously. The general accounting system generates the financial statements, and the managerial or subsidiary accounting system generates detailed management reports. The same financial information appears in both systems, with the subsidiary records breaking down the data into greater detail than what appears in the general ledger.

The costs of land and construction flow through the system in a similar manner, whether the construction is speculative or custom. The system accumulates costs on a house-by-house basis in the job cost subsidiary with separate categories or job cost accounts for each type of cost incurred. Costs are transferred to cost of sales accounts at closing or completion of contracts. An additional entry at closing records the revenues earned in the transaction.

The type of accounting system described in this book is commonly referred to as a double-entry system. In double-entry bookkeeping, each financial transaction affects at least two accounts within the five major accounting classifications: assets, liabilities, owners' equity, revenues, and expenses.

For example: When XYZ Excavating submits an invoice for work completed and accepted on unit #782 for $1,520, the following entries need to be recorded in the general accounting system and in the subsidiary system if the company is using the accrual method of accounting.

- When the invoice is received, two things happen:
  1. The house under construction, an asset, increases in value
  2. The company incurs an obligation, a liability, to pay the subcontractor for his services
- This transaction affects accounts in the general ledger system as well as the subsidiary systems:
  1. General ledger system
     Dr Direct construction cost (work in process inventory)—an asset for $1,520
     Cr Accounts payable—a liability for $1,520
  2. Job cost subsidiary system
     Dr Unit 782 under the job cost code of excavation for $1,520 to show the increase in cost
  3. Accounts payable subsidiary
     Cr The account for XYZ Excavating to show the subcontractor is owed $1,520
- When XYZ Excavating is paid, the following accounts are affected:
  1. Cash, an asset, is reduced
  2. Accounts payable, a liability, is decreased
- The transaction will be recorded as follows:
  1. General ledger system
     Dr Accounts payable—a liability for $1,520
     Cr Cash—an asset for $1,520
  2. Accounts payable subsidiary
     Dr The account for XYZ Excavating for $1520 to show that the subcontractor has been paid

All accounts in a subsidiary ledger must equal the balance shown in the general ledger. This means that every time an entry is made in a general ledger account that is supported by a subsidiary, an entry in the same amount needs to be made in one of the detailed accounts in the subsidiary system.

Before computers began to be utilized in data processing, transactions had to be recorded with separate steps in the general ledger and in the subsidiary ledgers. Computers facilitate making the entries in the subsidiary ledger because the programs are set up to do both entries at the same time. However, processes and procedures still need to be set in place to make sure that every transaction requiring entries in both general ledger and subsidiary ledgers is recorded in both places by filling out the necessary information requested on the screen to take the entry to the subsidiary.

Some computer systems will not allow the person doing the data entry to exit the transaction screen if a general ledger account supported by a subsidiary has been used and no details have been entered to take the transaction to the subsidiary ledger. Most computer systems, though, will allow entries into general ledger accounts supported by subsidiaries without requiring information for the subsidiary entry. Thus, processes need to be in place to ensure accurate recording of data to general ledger accounts as well as to subsidiary accounts when required, and general ledger accounts and their subsidiary ledgers need to be reconciled as part of the standard accounting procedures to ensure the integrity of the financial data.

Flow of Information

Financial information flows through an accounting system in the following sequence: from the journals—general and specials, such as cash, sales, payroll—to the general ledger to reports such as income statement, balance sheet, and cash flow.

Journals

Journals are books of original entry in which a bookkeeper records all of the company's financial transactions in chronological sequence. A bookkeeper can enter all financial transactions into the system through the general journal. However, to facilitate bookkeeping, special journals are used to record payroll, sales, purchases, cash receipts, and cash disbursements.

General Journal

The general journal is a two dollar-column record—one debit column and one credit column—in which transactions are entered in chronological order (Figure 5–1). The date of the transaction, the accounts affected by the transaction, and a short description are recorded for each entry. The left dollar-column is to record debits; the right-dollar column is for credits. After the bookkeeper records debits and credits, he or she adds a brief explanation.

If the bookkeeper uses special journals, the general journal is used only to record special transactions, adjustments, and end-of-month entries that generally require no cash inflows or cash disbursements.

Special Journals

Special journals facilitate the journalizing or sequential entry of financial transactions. In contrast to the general journal, special journals may have more than two dollar-columns. A multicolumn format designates separate dollar-columns for frequently used accounts. The type of special journal and the account determines whether columns represent debits or credits. For example, the cash column in the cash receipts journal is a debit column, and the cash column in the cash disbursement journal is a credit column.

Entries in special journals do not require explanations as do entries in the general journal. Thus, the bookkeeper saves time when journalizing. The name of the special journal identifies the nature of the transactions being recorded because the bookkeeper records only like transactions in each special journal. The bookkeeper also saves considerable time posting from a special journal because he or she only has to post the total of each column at the end of the month.

Date	Description	Ref. No.	Dr.	Cr.

Note: Actual format must reflect the specific needs of each company and may vary from those shown here and in Figures 5-2, 5-4, and 5-6.

Figure 5-1. General Journal Format.

Generally, the last two dollar-columns in a special journal contain entries to accounts for which no special column has been designated. Each amount recorded in these columns must be posted individually. Transactions recorded in special journals include payroll, sales, purchases, cash receipts, and cash disbursements.

The above description represents a manual system. Few companies today are doing their books without using some type of computerized accounting software.

In a computerized system the principles remain the same. Transactions are entered into the system through the journals and the software provides different screens to enter different types of transactions. These special screens are the special journals used in a manual system. Every computerized system also has a special screen to make entries that in a manual system will be made to the general journal. Again, entries are made in chronological order, each entry representing a financial transaction.

Ledgers

Ledgers accumulate financial information by account. The bookkeeper first enters all financial information in chronological order in a journal. Then the bookkeeper transfers the financial information from the journal into the designated accounts in the general ledger and the applicable subsidiary ledgers. The process of transferring financial data from the journal to the ledgers is called posting. Figure 5–2 shows the levels of recording in the general ledger and subsidiary ledgers.

General Ledger

The general ledger mirrors the accounts listed in the chart of accounts. The general ledger provides data for the traditional financial statements and some management reports. Information in the general ledger usually is not detailed enough to help builders, remodelers, and developers make daily business decisions. However, it is useful in analyzing trends and

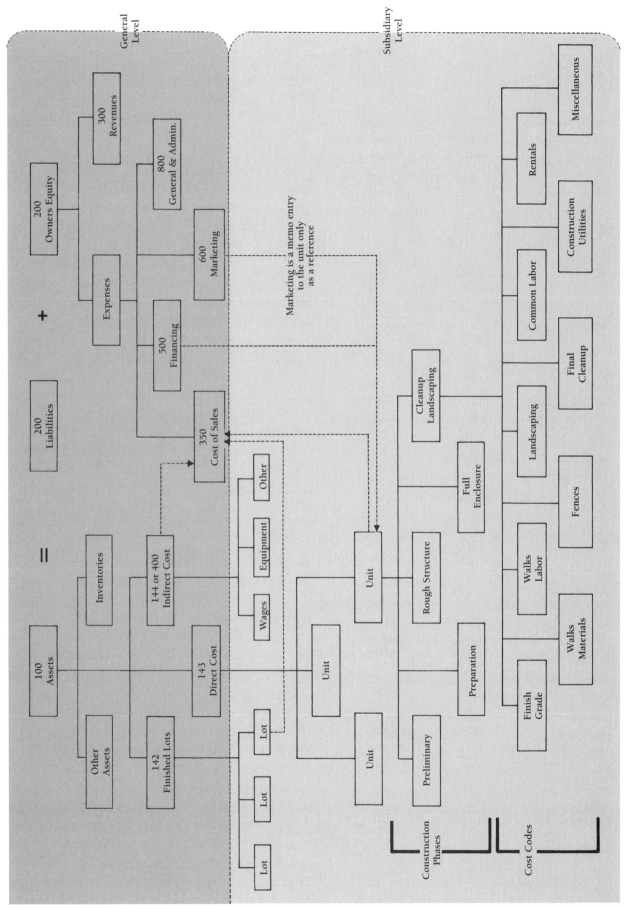

Figure 5–2. Levels of recording, general ledger and subsidiary ledgers.

overall profitability and in establishing goals and preparing plans for future performance.

Subsidiary Ledgers

A subsidiary ledger shows financial information in greater detail than does the general ledger because each subsidiary ledger provides a breakdown of a general ledger account. The total of all accounts in a subsidiary ledger must equal the balance of the general ledger account. The most commonly used subsidiary ledgers include:

- Accounts receivable
- Accounts payable
- Job cost, a breakdown of Account 143, direct construction cost

ACCOUNTS RECEIVABLE SUBSIDIARY

The accounts receivable subsidiary is a historical record of each person or company that owes money to a builder, remodeler, or developer; payments made; and outstanding balances as of a particular date. These transactions generally represent money due on contract from clients on jobs in progress.

ACCOUNTS PAYABLE SUBSIDIARY

The accounts payable subsidiary contains separate accounts for each supplier and subcontractor to whom the builder, remodeler, or developer owes money. When the bookkeeper receives the invoices, the bookkeeper records each credit to a supplier or subcontractor account in the accounts payable subsidiary when he or she enters the transaction in the journal. By recording payments or debits in the same manner, each account in the accounts payable subsidiary provides a historical record of all financial transactions with a particular supplier or subcontractor. The total of all accounts in the accounts payable subsidiary must equal the amount in the accounts payable general ledger account.

JOB COST SUBSIDIARY

One of the most important records in a homebuilding operation is the job cost subsidiary because it accumulates all construction costs on a house-by-house, parcel-by-parcel, or job-by-job basis. This subsidiary provides separate accounts for each unit of production and further classifies the costs for each house, job, or parcel into predetermined cost codes.

The size, needs, resources, and operating methods of a building, remodeling, or development firm dictate the degree of detail or number of cost codes in this subsidiary ledger. Reports generated from the job cost subsidiary, for example, provide builders, remodelers, and developers with a detailed knowledge of costs that enables them to (a) exercise control over their businesses and (b) make timely decisions on product mix, marketability, and pricing of future units or contracts. (Job cost accounting is discussed in greater detail in Chapter 9.)

The total of all accounts in the subsidiary ledger must equal the balance in the general ledger account. For example, at the end of each month, the bookkeeper prepares from the job cost subsidiary a schedule showing each unit under construction and the cost to date for each unit. The total construction cost from all the units under construction must equal the balance shown in the direct construction cost account in the general ledger.

Processing of Data

Journalizing

Journalizing is the first step in processing financial data. The bookkeeper enters data into the journals in chronological order on a daily basis or as he or she receives financial information.

At the end of each month, the bookkeeper adds all columns in each special journal, then adds the totals from all debit columns and the totals from all credit columns in each journal to verify that debits equal credits. Equal debits and credits only ensures that the journals balance, not that all entries are correct. Before posting the financial information to the ledger, the bookkeeper must make sure that all special journals balance.

Computerized accounting systems generally do not allow an entry to be completed until debits equal credits for each transaction, thus maintaining at all times the equality of debits and credits.

Posting

Posting is the process of recording totals from all journals to specific accounts in the general ledger. After posting, the bookkeeper computes new balances for each general ledger account and prepares a trial balance to ensure that debits and credits equal. Again, having debits and credits equal does not ensure that the amounts were posted to the right accounts.

The computerized accounting systems have, for all practical purposes, eliminated the process of posting. As transactions are recorded into the journals, the computer automatically completes the posting. Because most computerized systems will not allow a transaction not in balance (debits = credits) to be processed, as a general rule the general ledger accounts will not be out of balance as a result of human error in transferring numbers from journals to ledger accounts.

Adjusting Entries

At the end of every month, the accountant makes adjusting entries and reviews the trial balance before preparing the financial statements. Typical adjusting entries record depreciation of fixed assets, amortization of intangible assets such as organization costs, and allocation of indirect construction costs between costs of sales and inventory. At this time, the accountant will also correct any mistakes and miscoding of data that become apparent while reviewing the trial balance and records prepared by the bookkeeper. Adjusting entries could be made monthly, quarterly, bi-annually, or annually.

Closing Entries

At the end of an accounting year, the accountant prepares closing entries. Closing entries summarize in the owners' equity account the net income or net loss for the year. The accountant transfers the balances of the revenue and expense accounts to owners' equity. This transfer leaves the revenue and expense accounts with zero balances at the start of the new accounting year so that the accounts will accumulate only the amounts for the new period. The accountant generally will prepare closing entries when he or she gets ready to review, close, and prepare financial and managerial reports for the accounting period just ended.

Computerized accounting systems automatically do the closing entries when prompted, that is, at the end of the accounting period.

Office Filing Procedures

Filing procedures are often overlooked or given little attention until an invoice, contract, or other important document cannot be found. When setting up a filing system for a building, remodeling, or development business, you should consider retrieval time a top priority.

Organize job files with subfiles that allow you to classify the paperwork into logical groups such as permits, correspondence, customer selections, and purchase orders. For visibility, you can use color tabs to identify the types of files and numbered stickers to identify all files relating to a particular job. For example, given that job 5412 has four file folders, all four files would have a sticker with the number 5412 in the left upper corner to indicate that the files are for that job. Assigning one color to each type of file would help in quickly retrieving documents. For example, on the right upper corner of each folder, a color tab indicates it is one of the following types of files:

- Red   permits
- Blue   correspondence
- Green   customer selections
- Orange   purchase orders

Therefore, the permit file folder for job 5412 will have a sticker with that number and a red tab to identify the folder as the permit file.

A number of activities in a building, remodeling, or land development firm may require separate sets of files. The example given above is a typical way to organize job information.

Retrieval time also is the key for setting up a filing system for invoices from subcontractors and suppliers. Invoices generally require a dual filing system, one file for open or unpaid invoices and one for paid invoices. How you group invoices depends on how you process payments. Sometimes copies of invoices must be submitted with individual draw requests for each house, remodeling job, or lot. You should group such invoices by job until you process and pay them. Some invoices need not accompany draw requests. You can keep such open invoices (until you process and pay them) in alphabetical order in a series of files labeled with the letters of the alphabet. For paid invoices you should maintain a separate file folder for each subcontractor and supplier and file each company invoice (with a copy of your payment check attached) in reverse chronological order in that company's file. Some builders, remodelers, and developers cross file their invoices by house, job, or lot number. However, that duplication of effort is unnecessary.

Because more than one person uses a company's filing system, it must be easy to understand and simple to use.

CHAPTER 6

Internal Control

Objectives and Requirements

Every builder, remodeler, or developer should establish a system of internal control. The purpose of the internal control system is to protect the assets of the company (things of value owned by the company such as cash, inventories, equipment) and ensure that the accounting records accurately reflect the economic transactions that took place during a given period of time and that the value of the assets is accurately presented.

To achieve these objectives, four basic functions must be present in the internal control system:

1. Authorization: Every financial transaction must be authorized by a manager prior to execution.
2. Record-keeping: Financial transactions must be recorded in a timely manner.
3. Custodianship: Only authorized employees should have access to the company's assets. In addition, the company's assets should be reconciled periodically with the accounting records to ensure proper and authorized use of the assets.
4. Operations: Policies and procedures need to be set in place to ensure that operations will be carried out properly.

The segregation of these functions is the essence of any internal control system because it reduces the likelihood of fraud, theft, or mismanagement within a company. In many small companies it is almost impossible to have full segregation of these functions. If this is the case, explore the possibility of insuring or bonding employees, particularly if they have easy access to assets, can authorize financial transactions, and have access to the accounting records.

Authorization

The builder, remodeler, or developer should properly authorize all financial transactions and clearly identify the person or people responsible for each type of transaction. Some companies, especially large ones, may have different levels of authority. For instance, a superintendent may buy up to $300 worth of lumber or miscellaneous tools but someone else (such as the owner or construction manager) would have to approve a larger order.

Record-keeping

The actual recording of financial transactions in the accounting system is known as record-keeping. The person in charge of the record-keeping should have no authority to purchase or authorize financial transactions. By the same token, employees authorizing financial transactions should have NO access to the accounting records. Builders, remodelers, and developers generally tend to be very lax in providing adequate security for their accounting records.

Even though computers are generally accessible to most employees in a company, all accounting software systems provide users with passwords to different areas of the system to protect the data from being change by an unauthorized employee. Make sure proper passwords are set up to protect the data entry process.

Custodianship

A custodian directly supervises the assets of a company. The person who acts as custodian should never have access to the company's actual records or be given the power to authorize the use of the assets. The custodian may allow only authorized personnel to use the assets. For example, one person in the company (possibly the secretary) should have possession of all large electric tools owned by the company and check them out only to authorized personnel, keep track of who has them, and make sure the borrowers return the tools in good condition.

The major and most illusive asset of the company is cash. The segregation of authorizing transactions, record-keeping , and custodianship is critical to the safeguarding of cash. In a small company in which it is difficult to achieve this segregation of functions, the owner should maintain custodianship of the cash by retaining signature privileges in all bank accounts and reviewing monthly bank statements. If it becomes too cumbersome or time-consuming, the owner could choose to have two signatures on the checks and assign one or more employees to that task. In any case, it is always advisable to bond employees who have signature privileges or who work in the accounting department.

Policies and Procedures

Carrying out the goals and objectives of a company involves implementing policies and procedures. The quality of a firm's employees has a great impact on the successful use of the internal control system. But, no matter how competent they are, they must be adequately supervised. Authorization procedures should require the owner or a field employee to verify (a) delivery and status of materials and (b) completion of work and the quality of that work prior to payment of invoices. A small-volume firm may have an accountant or CPA periodically review the accounting records to ensure proper procedures are being followed.

Responsibility for designing and implementing an internal control system rests with the owner or a top manager. The factors discussed in the following paragraphs directly influence the control procedures needed by a particular firm.

Size. The size of the business and the number of employees have a direct bearing on any system of internal control. A business requires standard procedures to be able to trace lines of responsibility. These procedures are especially necessary as a business expands. Even though authorization to perform a function might be delegated to an employee, the owners or managers are ultimately responsible for the company's financial status. Therefore the builder, remodeler, or developer must establish policies and procedures to ensure that all operations are carried out properly.

The larger the business, the more structured and detailed the internal control system should be. In a small firm in which adequate segregation of functions might prove impossible, builders, remodelers, and developers need to be aware of the implications of delegating more than one of the four basic functions (record-keeping, custodianship, authorization, and implementation) to the same employee. The risk of fraud or misappropriation of assets increases. As mentioned previously, the owner has the option of bonding the employee and insuring against any losses caused by theft or fraud.

Management Style. The management style of a company will impact internal control. As owners delegate more responsibilities to employees, they need to increase and standardize procedures to maintain adequate control of their operations. Hands-on involvement produces the tightest control.

Cost. You should evaluate the cost of learning and using a procedure against the procedure's benefits. When the cost exceeds the benefits, you should explore the alternatives and either eliminate the procedure or try a different approach.

Method of Collecting Financial Information. Computers have made segregation of the bookkeeping function more difficult because normally one person enters data in both the general and the subsidiary ledgers, and all journals and ledgers are stored on the same disk so that the bookkeeper can access all records easily. Implementing efficient procedures with computers requires going beyond traditional methods used in a manual bookkeeping system. Computer systems provide the use of passwords to access different areas of the program. Builders, remodelers, and developers need to be

aware of this capability and protect different segments of the accounting records.

In addition to the general internal control system, builders, remodelers, or developers must establish procedures to maintain proper control over five basic business activities:

- Sales (the accumulated actual sales, the receivable that is created as a result of the sale, and the cash receipts or collection of accounts)
- Purchasing (the ordering of material or services required, the payables, and the cash paid out for the materials and services)
- Production and inventories (the actual construction process and the management of inventories)
- Personnel and payroll (the procedures to calculate, approve, and disburse paychecks to all employees)
- Property, plant, and equipment maintenance (overseeing the use of all property and equipment owned by the company)

Cash Management and Control

Cash management requires special attention because cash, other than perhaps inventory, is an organization's most important asset. Therefore the builder, remodeler, or developer must follow certain guidelines for handling each receipt and disbursement of cash. This section contains specific guidelines and procedures to help a builder, remodeler, or developer safeguard the company's cash against theft.

Checking Account Procedures

Cash Balance Control

Usually the bookkeeper is responsible for keeping the cash running balance in either the check register or on the check stubs. A check register is a list of the checks written and deposits made into an account. The register also should include all debits and credits made by the bank, such as service charges and interest earned. These charges and credits must be added or subtracted after every transaction to maintain a correct running balance. Computer systems can maintain a detailed check register with a running cash balance. The paragraphs that follow describe how to maintain control of your cash balance.

Deposits. Checks paid to the company should always be deposited. Establish a written policy to require that all funds received, whether in cash or by check, be deposited into the company's checking account as quickly as possible after they are received. This policy ensures that you can account for all funds received.

Withdrawals. Each cash withdrawal requires a check properly identifying the payee and the reason for the disbursement. Company policy should prohibit checks written to "Cash" because you may not be able to identify the payee and the validity of the disbursement at a later date.

Even in large companies, check signing should remain the responsibility of the owner or treasurer. In businesses with more than one principal or partner, a two-signature requirement is common. However, although the two signatures provide for checks and balances, it also lengthens the check-writing process. Bonding signators and accounting personnel is always a good option and relatively inexpensive for the protection it provides.

Numerical Sequence of Checks. Once you have instituted a policy of making all cash disbursements by check, the next point of control is the numerical sequence of the checks. Prenumbered checks ensure accountability of all checks. Record voided checks in the check register, identify them as voided, cut off the signature area, and keep them on file to maintain the accountability of all checks. A quick review of the numerical sequence in the check register will verify that all checks have been accounted for. This practice helps ensure that all withdrawals are recorded and deducted from the cash balance.

Avoid allowing blank checks to go out of the office. All payments should originate at the company's office. When it becomes necessary to take a blank check out of the office, record the check number, the person taking the check, and the reason for tak-

ing the check in a special register to facilitate follow up. Make sure the withdrawal is recorded in the system as soon as possible.

Bank Reconciliation. The bank reconciliation helps control and manage the cash by verifying the accuracy of the cash balance, deposits, checks, and other debits and credits shown in the company's books and the banks records.

The back side of a bank statement usually provides a reconciliation form for customer use. The format is the same as or similar to the format presented in this chapter. Today, most computerized accounting systems provide a bank reconciliation process.

To carry out a reconciliation, follow the procedures listed below:

- Have on hand the previous month's reconciliation, the current bank statement, the canceled checks, other documentation included with the bank statement, and the check register or check stubs.
- Verify deposits shown in the check register against those shown in the bank statement.
- List deposits made after the bank statement's closing date.
- Organize canceled checks in numerical sequence.
- Compare the canceled checks with the list of outstanding checks on the previous month's bank reconciliation, and list checks that are still outstanding.
- Verify amounts on canceled checks against recorded amounts in the check register. Put a check mark by the verified, recorded amounts. Specifically watch for mistakes in the last two digits or transposition of numbers. Keep in mind that banks also make mistakes when processing checks.
- List outstanding checks from the period covered in the reconciliation.
- List and analyze charges or credits issued by the bank that are not recorded in the check register.
- Prepare the reconciliation statement as shown in Figure 6–1.

The reconciliation statement should list:

- The bank balance for the account
- Outstanding deposits

Bank Balance	$1,589.10
Plus deposits in transit	249.00
Total	$1,838.10
Less outstanding checks	536.50
Adjusted bank balance	$1,301.60*
Book balance	$1,421.60
Credits issued by bank	0.00
Charges issued by bank	
Check order—printing	105.00
Service charge	15.00
Adjusted book balance	$1,301.60*

List of Outstanding Checks

Check Number	Amount
1031	$151.00
1042	24.50
1043	361.00
Total	$536.50

*The adjusted balance and the adjusted book balance must be equal if the account is to be reconciled.

Figure 6-1. Bank reconciliation statement January 31, 19XX.

- Outstanding checks
- The check register balance
- Credits or charges made by the bank and not previously recorded in the check register

If any bank charge, credit, or other transaction is not yet recorded in the accounting system, you should prepare a journal entry to record it. In case of a discrepancy between the bank statement and the check register balance, you should:

- Confirm that old outstanding checks have been included in the list of outstanding checks.
- Verify amounts written on checks against amounts posted in the check register.
- Verify the amount shown on each check against the amount shown in the bank statement.
- Check for transposition of numbers.
- Identify deposits in transit.
- Check for an unexpected bank credit or charge.
- Check for duplicated entries in the check register or bank statement.
- Verify that all deposits have been credited to the right account and are shown in the bank statement. This common bank error often occurs when a business has more than one account in the same bank.
- Check for mathematical errors.

The preceding checklist contains some of the most common causes for discrepancies, but it is by no means complete. If all else fails in the reconciliation attempt, call the company's accountant or enlist the help of the bank bookkeeping staff. After the reconciliation the bank balance and the balance in the accounting records must always be the same.

Cash Receipts and Disbursements

The control function safeguards the company's cash through proper administration and use of the firm's cash resources. You must establish procedures to ensure the following:

- All money received is properly accounted for.
- Enough cash is available to make the necessary disbursements.
- Disbursements are legitimate, necessary, and properly authorized.
- The checking account contains no idle, excess cash.

To prevent the potential problems of misappropriation of funds, kickbacks, and rerouting of checks, delegate authority carefully. To provide a system of checks and balances, whenever possible assign different individuals to perform each of the following functions or consider insuring or bonding anyone who handles more than one of them:

- Receive and safeguard cash
- Purchase materials and services
- Record transactions in the general ledger
- Record transactions in the subsidiary ledger(s)
- Approve disbursements
- Sign checks

The person signing checks should use the following procedures:

- Review supporting documents such as invoices, purchase orders, and statements.
- Verify that the payee is correct and determine whether the check is to be sent to the address on the invoice and if not, why not.

- Verify the payee and the amount of checks that are not paying an invoice, for example, payroll, rent, and travel advances.
- Account for all checks by reviewing their numerical sequence.
- Generally ascertain that disbursements are reasonable.

After disbursements are made, mark supporting documents "paid" to avoid inadvertently repaying them. File paid invoices by vendor to facilitate retrieval and provide a record of transactions with each vendor.

Petty Cash

A company may require a petty cash fund when small disbursements are frequent. This fund must be used strictly for small disbursements, and receipts must always substantiate these transactions.

Procedures for setting up and controlling a petty cash fund are:

- Establish the fund with a check for $100 to $200, payable to petty cash and the person who will handle the petty cash.
- Cash the check.
- Disburse the money as necessary, and replace the cash with receipts. (Available cash plus receipts on hand must always equal the original petty cash fund balance.)
- When the fund needs to be replenished, make out a check payable to petty cash and the person handling the petty cash for the total amount of receipts to restore the fund to its original balance.
- Mark "paid" on petty cash receipts that are reimbursed by the fund. This practice prevents fraudulent reuse of the receipts.

Loan Administration

Proper administration of loans ensures smooth disbursements of loan funds and it helps to maintain a good and on-going working relationship with financial institutions. Administering a loan in a hap-

hazard manner can jeopardize your relationship with the lender.

Delegate Responsibility

The first step in a loan administration program is to delegate the responsibility to one individual. This person must become quite familiar with the requirements in the loan agreement and incorporate key dates in a tickler file to ensure that the firm meets established datelines.

Learn and Follow Procedures

The next step is to clearly understand and follow the disbursement procedures. Because generally the loan documents do not outline the disbursement procedures, the person who administers the company loans needs to contact the financial institution.

- How often can disbursements be made (monthly, semimonthly, weekly)?
- What is the lead time from submission of an application for a draw to disbursement?
- What are the bottleneck dates (the dates when most other borrowers are submitting their draws and lead times for the bank to issue funds tend to be longer)?
- What format is to be used? Does the company need to submit a special form?
- What documentation does the company need to supply? Surveys, engineering reports, copies of invoices?

Each financial institution has slightly different requirements and each type of loan has different disbursement procedures. Even when loans are renewed with the same financial institution, disbursement procedures need to be reviewed to ensure that procedures have not changed.

Timely disbursements of funds is one of the keys to the smooth operation of a business. Presentation of the request for funds or draws is almost as important as the presentation to obtain the loan. If you have to submit copies of invoices, make sure that all copies are legible and that invoices follow the same order in which they appear on the loan request form. Preferably, type all forms in the draw request package and make sure the package is clean, organized, and has a professional look.

Account for the Funds

The third consideration in loan administration is to maintain accountability of the funds. In the NAHB Chart of Accounts, Account 126, due on construction and development loans, and Account 252, acquisition, development, and construction loans payable, provide for easy assessment of loan status. Signing the loan agreement establishes the obligation; credit the loan to Account 252. At the same time debit the loan to Account 126 to establish the dollars available through the loan. Every time a draw is made, credit Account 126 to reduce the balance to draw on the loan. The difference between these two accounts is the total amount drawn to date or the amount due the financial institution at any given time. The balance on Account 126 will tell you how much is left to draw from the loan.

The loan administrator should make periodic assessments as to whether the loan will be paid on the due date. He or she must allow enough time, prior to the due date, to prepare documentation, exercise extension options, or negotiate new extensions if the company will not meet the due date.

Estimating and Purchasing

The estimating, purchasing, and cost control functions are so interrelated that each function must use the same structure to ensure efficient operation of a building, remodeling, or development firm.

The thrust of any cost control system is the comparison between projected costs or estimates and actual costs. Unless the estimates are prepared using the same structure used to accumulate actual cost, meaningful comparison between the estimate and the actual costs cannot be made.

To make such comparisons possible, the estimate prepared for pricing a project must reflect the purchasing units in order to translate the estimate into purchase orders or list of materials and services needed for the job. The estimating and purchasing phase of the construction process, and the way in which materials and labor are ordered, generally follows the construction sequence. Therefore, it makes sense to organize the job cost accounts to follow the construction sequence. When the cost codes follow the construction sequence, integration of the invoice approval process with the scheduling system is facilitated.

As invoices come in, they can be compared with the estimate to make sure the amount to be paid is the amount that should be paid. Providing a uniform structure for estimating, purchasing, and accounting can save time, increase the accuracy of the estimating process, and establish a cost control system that leads to increased profits.

Coordination With the Accounting System

The accounting system measures and accumulates in cost codes the actual costs incurred during the construction process. A common problem in developing a job cost chart of accounts is the temptation to include too many accounts. Builders who break down cost codes into minute components end up with too much detail, which in most cases is irrelevant. Each cost code should represent a control point that generally equates to a pay point.

The following guidelines are helpful when developing a job cost chart of accounts:

- Make it simple. Avoid more cost codes than you absolutely need.
- Coordinate the job cost codes with the way you estimate, purchase, and pay your suppliers and subcontractors.
- Do not assign more than one vendor to a cost code.
- Each cost code should represent one invoice whenever possible.

- Follow the construction sequence to be able to coordinate the invoice approval process with the scheduling system.
- Make sure the cost codes reflect the way you build.
- Break down the cost classification into material and labor only if you supply the material and subcontract just the labor. Otherwise, separate the contract amount into cost codes that reflect the amounts to be paid at each draw.

Appendix E provides an example of a job cost chart of accounts. Use this example only as a general guide. Each company needs to generate its own chart based on the guidelines outlined above.

CHAPTER 7

Financial Reports

As previously discussed, the bookkeeper or accountant prepares the balance sheet and the income statement, generally called financial statements, from the financial data accumulated by the accounting system.

The most important criteria for designing or preparing other reports are its usefulness as a historical record of the business operations and as a decision-making tool affecting future company operations. To evaluate the usefulness of a report, compare the cost of preparation with the benefits derived from the report.

A report's usefulness increases considerably when it compares historical data with a plan or budget, with figures from previous periods, and/or with industry figures. To ensure comparability, the same methods and principles must be used to accumulate data from period to period. Consider the following guidelines when preparing financial reports:

- Reports should be easy to read and understand.
- Reports should indicate the data source.
- Deviations from a plan or budget must be highlighted.
- Actual and planned or budgeted figures must be comparable.

- Reports for owners of small companies should contain detailed data. In large companies, reports for company owners and top managers should contain summary data. Lower level managers get reports with detailed data backing up the summarized reports.
- Reports should be timely so that a builder, remodeler, or developer can take action to correct any problems the reports reveal.
- Information in the reports should be accurate and reliable.
- Reports should be produced in standardized formats whenever possible.

Balance Sheet and Income Statement

To prepare a balance sheet and an income statement, the balances shown in the general ledger accounts are grouped into standard formats generally accepted by the accounting and financial professions. These statements can be made more useful by relating them to each other, comparing results from the present period with results from prior periods and with industry standards. The understanding of the financial information as presented on these two statements can also be enhanced by calculating ratios.

The accounting equation is represented by the financial statements as the statements relate to one another:

Balance Sheet:
Assets = Liabilities + Owners' Equity

Income Statement:
Revenues − Cost and Expenses =
Net Income or Net Loss

The net income or loss is then reflected in the balance sheet in the owners' equity section.

Balance Sheet

The balance sheet represents a company's financial position on a specific date—generally the end of a month, quarter, or year (see table below). It reflects the value of the firm's assets on a cost basis and identifies who has current claims to the assets—creditors or owners—and the amounts of those claims on the date that appears on the statement.

XYZ Home Building Company
Balance Sheet
December 31, 20XX

ASSETS	
Current Assets:	
Cash	$985,000
Inventories—Land	$10,200,000
Inventories—Work in Proces	$4,500,000
Total Current Assets	**$15,685,000**
Other Assets	$1,450,000
TOTAL ASSETS	**$17,135,000**
LIABILITIES & OWNERS' EQUITY	
Liabilities:	
Current Liabilities	$9,200,000
Long-term Liabilities	$4,300,000
Total Liabilities	**$13,500,000**
Owners' Equity	$3,635,000
TOTAL LIABILITIES & OWNERS' EQUITY	**$17,135,000**

Each financial transaction affects the company's financial condition. Because the balance sheet is current only as of the date indicated on its heading, you must understand and interpret it as a static report.

Builders, remodelers, and developers use the balance sheet primarily to evaluate the company's financial strength, liquidity, and leverage. The balance sheet provides general information for developing company plans and goals and it allows outsiders to determine the risk factor for loans and investments.

A trend analysis or comparative analysis of more than one balance sheet can help identify the company's overall operating philosophy, structural changes, and liquidity patterns. Examined in conjunction with the income statement, a balance sheet reveals other important information, such as how effectively the company's resources are being used, the status of investments in land and inventories, rate of return on assets and owners' equity, and leverage.

Assets

Assets are items of value owned by a company in tangible form (such as cash, equipment, and land) or in the form of claims or future benefits (such as prepaid insurance, accounts receivable, and amounts due on construction loans).

Assets are generally represented by debit balances in the accounting system. Therefore, a debit entry increases the asset and a credit entry decreases the asset. In the NAHB Chart of Accounts, assets are identified by the 1000 series.

Liabilities

Liabilities are a company's obligations to third parties—such as accounts payable, loans payable, and payroll taxes payable. In other words, liabilities represent claims to the assets of the firm by outsiders.

Liabilities are generally represented by credit balances. Therefore, a debit to a liability account decreases the liability and a credit increases the liability. In the NAHB Chart of Accounts, liabilities are identified by the 2000 series.

Owners' Equity

Owners' equity represents the claims that the owners of a business have on the company's assets. Owners' equity consists of two basic elements: the owners' investment (capital stock) and retained earnings (the accumulation of profits or losses from operations). On the balance sheet, the retained earnings account reflects the accumulation of a firm's net profit or losses since the time the business was established less any withdrawals by the owners.

Owners' equity accounts usually carry a credit balance unless these accounts are showing a deficit. In the case of a deficit, the owners' equity accounts are represented by a debit balance. In the NAHB Chart of Accounts, owners' equity accounts are identified in the 2000 series.

Income Statement

The income statement summarizes the revenues, cost of sales, and operating expenses for a period of time—a month, quarter, or a year—with net income or net loss reflecting the result of the company's operations for the period (see table below). Net income or net loss becomes part of the balance sheet by increasing or decreasing the owners' equity for the period and thus keeping the accounting equation equal or balanced.

Revenues

Revenues represent the consideration received or earned for providing goods and services to a third party. Revenues are represented by credit balances in the accounting system because they increase the owners' equity.

Revenues are usually presented as a lump sum in the income statement. However, if a business provides more than one type of product or service,

XYZ Home Building Company
Income Statement
For year ended 20XX

Revenues:	
Sales—Single family	$29,650,000
Cost of Sales:	
Land	$3,700,000
Direct Cost	$17,150,000
Total Cost of Sales	$20,850,000
Gross Profit	**$8,800,000**
Operating Expenses:	
Indirect Construction Cost	$860,000
Financing Expenses	$1,560,000
Sales & Marketing	$2,200,000
General & Administrative	$1,425,000
Total Operating Expenses	$6,045,000
Net Operating Income	**$2,755,000**

each source of revenue should be identified. For example:

- Sales of single-family speculative homes
- Sales of single family, custom-designed homes
- Sales of developed lots
- Remodeling
- Rental of construction equipment

If different types of revenues are lumped together, there is no way to analyze how well each revenue area is performing, making it very difficult to identify areas that might require improvement.

Cost of Sales

Cost of sales represents all costs associated with the products sold by a business. Cost adds value to the product. In contrast, expenses are necessary for the day-to-day operation of a business but do not add value to the product.

In a homebuilding, remodeling, or land development operation, cost of sales includes cost of land, land development, and construction cost. Construc-

tion costs are classified into two major categories, direct and indirect, and include materials, labor, and all other costs associated with the building process.

DIRECT CONSTRUCTION COST

Direct construction cost includes the cost of the sticks and bricks and the labor to put them up. The direct cost can always be traced to a particular project, unit of construction, remodeling job, or parcel of land.

INDIRECT CONSTRUCTION COST

The indirect construction costs include costs incurred during the construction process that cannot be directly assigned to a particular unit of construction. Examples of indirect construction costs include the costs of supervision, field offices, operation of construction trucks, warehousing of construction materials, and temporary utilities.

The term *overhead* is often used to describe this type of cost. Exercise caution when using this term, however, because *overhead* can rightfully include expenses related to financing and sales and marketing of the product as well as general and administrative expenses. Whenever the term *overhead* is used, it is necessary to clarify which types of cost and/or expenses are included.

ABSORPTION COSTING

Absorption costing requires that both direct cost and indirect cost be part of the total cost of each unit of production. Because indirect construction costs cannot be directly related to a unit of production, a proportional share of the cost is allocated to each unit, job, or lot. Absorption costing combines the unit's, job's, or lot's proportional share of indirect construction cost with its direct construction cost to determine the total cost of the unit, job, or lot. The indirect costs are accumulated in an inventory (asset) account (1440). This account requires a subsidiary to be able to keep track of each type of cost in this major classification. The subsidiary ledger operates the same as other subsidiaries in the accounting system. The Internal Revenue Service requires that inventories and cost of sales be valued according to the absorption costing method.

An alternate method can be used to facilitate the tracking and control of indirect construction costs. Instead of accumulating the indirect costs in an inventory (asset) account with a subsidiary, these costs could be treated as operating expenses and accumulated in the 4000 series of accounts, thus facilitating the evaluation of each of the components in this classification. The control of these expenses is facilitated because each account is part of the general ledger. This method eliminates the requirement of an additional subsidiary. The indirect costs associated with the production function can then be evaluated in a similar fashion as the finance, sales and marketing, and administrative functions.

It is important to remember that, to comply with external reporting requirements and Internal Revenue Service regulations, the proportional portion of the cost in the 4000 series that relates to the work in process inventory needs to be allocated to an inventory account (1440). This allocation does not require a detailed breakdown of the type of costs because the system maintains the details in the 4000 series.

Allocation of Indirect Construction Costs

To allocate indirect costs as construction, remodeling, or development progresses, a rate must be selected based on budgeted indirect cost and the anticipated level of production. This allocation is based on estimates; thus, most likely the allocated amount will not match exactly the actual cost. At year's end the accountant or CPA will reconcile the actual cost to the allocated amount.

Prepare a budget or plan for all the indirect costs to be incurred in the accounting year. The total of the budget or plan is the budgeted indirect cost. Based on the projected sales for the same period, estimate the number of units, jobs, or lots to be built or developed. This number will be the anticipated level of production.

The level of production can be expressed in a number of different ways, such as number of units, volume of dollars of direct construction cost, or direct labor hours. Each method has its advantages and drawbacks; therefore, you need to select a method that best suits your company's way of doing business.

For example, a production builder or a developer might express production level by number of units or lots:

Projected indirect cost for the year	$525,000
Projected volume in units	250
Allocation per unit ($525,000/250)	$2,100

Under this method, indirect construction cost of $2,100 is added to the total cost of each house built during the year.

In a business with a diversified product line—for example, a builder who does some remodeling—distribution of direct cost to all units or jobs on an even basis would not be equitable. Larger projects take longer to build and should have a larger share of the indirect construction cost. In businesses with their own crews, expressing production level by labor hours or direct construction cost becomes a more effective way of allocating the indirect construction cost:

Projected indirect construction cost $525,000
Projected direct construction cost $15,750,000
Ratio of $525,000/$15,750,000   3.3%

For each dollar of direct cost spent, 3.3 cents of indirect cost must be added to the total cost of the unit. The larger or more costly the house, remodeling job, or developed lot, the larger the share of indirect cost:

Model A, unit 205

Cost of land	$18,000
Direct construction cost	$95,500
Indirect construction cost of 3.3%	$3,151.50
Total cost of house	$116,651.50

Model B, unit 125

Cost of land	$25,250
Direct construction cost	$115,950
Indirect construction cost of 3.3%	$3,826
Total cost of house	$145,026

Bear in mind that the entry to allocate indirect construction costs is not required on an on-going basis, particularly when the alternate method of tracking these costs in the 4000 series of accounts is used. The allocation can be done on a monthly, quarterly, or annual basis or when reporting to third parties requiring compliance with the absorption method of accounting. Generally the CPA or accountant will be responsible for making the allocation entry into the system.

In a development company the nature and allocation of indirect construction cost would vary depending on the size and length of the project. In large developments, a number of items are incorporated into the community, such as recreational facilities, open spaces, and other amenities and impact fees that would be considered indirect costs in addition to the traditional indirect construction costs of supervision, temporary utilities, field offices, and the like. In addition, the development process could extend beyond a year, in which case you need to estimate the total indirect cost for the entire life of the development process to determine the proper allocation to each finished lot.

You can use various criteria to make the actual allocation. For example, you could divide the total indirect cost by the number of finished lots and allocate the same amount to each lot. Another common method of allocating indirect costs to finished lots is to use the market value of the development. In this instance you would compare the total market value of the development with the total indirect costs to determine a ratio. For example, the total market value of a development is $2.5 million. The indirect costs for the project total $250,000. The ratio of indirect cost to market value is 10 percent. Therefore $2,500 of indirect costs need to be added to the cost of each lot.

Unless a remodeling company chooses to use the completed contract method of income recognition, it need not be concerned with allocation of indirect construction cost. For a remodeler that recognizes revenues as he or she collects on contracts, indirect construction costs become period costs that can be charged off in the period in which they are incurred. Series 4000 in the NAHB Chart of Accounts handles indirect construction costs as period costs. If the remodeler using the completed contract method recognizes revenue only when the contract is complete, construction costs accumulate in an inventory account until completion. At completion, the remodeler recognizes construction costs as cost of sales with a proportional share of indirect construction costs. He or she must allocate the indirect cost to all jobs. Because the types and sizes of remodeling jobs are so diverse, the best method of allocation is the ratio of indirect cost to total construction cost.

Operating Expenses

Operating expenses are necessary expenditures incurred in day-to-day business operations. They are classified into three major categories: financing, sales and marketing, and general and administrative.

Financing Expenses

Financing expenses is a major line item in any building, remodeling, or development company. It includes interest, points, and fees paid in relation to borrowing or commitments to borrow. Because building, remodeling, and development businesses are usually operating on borrowed money, financing expenses can become significant. You need to distinguish between development and construction loans, commitments for permanent financing, points, other fees paid at closings, and funds borrowed for operating capital.

Currently all construction financing expenses must be added to the cost of units built—a process called capitalization. You must accumulate and include as inventory any interest paid on construction loans during the construction phase—whether it relates to land development or direct construction costs. Interest incurred on completed units or model homes can be expensed when incurred.

Other financing expenses are treated as regular expenses, regardless of operational structure. The 5000 series of the NAHB Chart of Accounts contains a breakdown for financing expenses.

Again, there is an alternate method of dealing with financing expenses to facilitate analysis and control of this expense. Interim financing expenses can also be accumulated in the expense classification, series 5000, and an adjusting entry can be made when reporting to third parties requiring the capitalization rule. This will provide management with the total cost of financing the production operation for a given period of time.

Interest rates are set by external economic forces, and they largely control financing expenses. However, construction financing expenses are affected by time. Therefore, efficient construction, remodeling, and development schedules help to control this expense, as does good management of speculative inventory units. You should monitor financing expenses closely so that prices of products and services reflect rate increases or decreases. Also monitor interest rates to evaluate future growth and to determine long-range plans, future marketability, and pricing policies.

Sales and Marketing Expenses

This group of expenses measures the effectiveness of the marketing and sales efforts. The structure of the sales and marketing function will impact your abil-ity to control these expenses. If a company has no in-house sales force, the expense is somewhat determined by the prevailing commission rate in the area.

An in-house sales force allows for more control over the sales and marketing expenses. A strong economy requires fewer marketing dollars, whereas hard economic times tend to require a larger share of gross margin dollars for creative marketing approaches.

Series 6000 in the NAHB Chart of Accounts classifies sales and marketing expenses into different types of expenditures.

General and Administrative Expenses

General and administrative expenses usually include expenses related to running the office, such as salaries of administrative personnel and officers, rent, supplies, insurance, licenses, travel and entertainment, educational programs, and professional fees. These types of expenses should be accumulated so that each account measures the type of expense it represents. Managers can then use the account reports to make decisions to curtail or expand the expense item. Some of these expenses can be subject to the capitalization rule required by the Internal Revenue Service. Seek the advice of a tax expert to make sure that the necessary adjustments are made when preparing the income tax return.

Series 8000 of the NAHB Chart of Accounts presents a detailed list of the different types of expenses classified under this series. The Chart of Accounts can be expanded as necessary to meet the needs of the individual business.

Other Income and Expenses

These line items are reserved to report income and expenses for items that do not relate to the main economic activity of the business or for extraordinary transactions that are not part of the everyday operation of the business. An example is a gain or loss realized on the sale of office equipment. Series 9000 in the NAHB Chart of Accounts represents this "other" category.

CHAPTER 8

Financial Analysis

Financial analysis is the analytical review of financial information accumulated in the accounting system and reported in financial statements. Financial analysis helps identify trends and compare the data in the financial reports with predetermined goals, industry standards, and data from prior periods. These comparisons enable the builder, remodeler, and developer to measure financial strength, the efficiency of the business operation, and the return on investment. Through financial analysis, problems or areas needing improvement can be isolated, thus helping reach the ultimate goal of maximizing profits in the long-term and achieving the best return on owners' investments.

This chapter discusses how financial analysis can help business owners improve their operations.

Gross Profit Analysis

Gross profit is the difference between sales and cost of sales, with cost of sales including the lot cost and the direct construction cost.

$$\text{Gross Profit} = \text{Sales} - \text{Cost of Sales}$$

The gross profit ratio can be obtained by dividing sales into gross profit.

$$\text{Gross Profit Ratio} = \frac{\text{Gross Profit}}{\text{Sales}}$$

Gross profit represents the first line of defense against poor financial performance. It measures the overall ability of the business to cover operating expenses. If a builder, remodeler, or developer does not attain an adequate gross profit ratio, the likelihood of obtaining good net profits is greatly reduced.

A look at gross profit per model, unit, remodeling job, or lot shows the contribution that each model, unit, remodeling job, or lot makes toward the operating expenses and profit of the company.

The gross profit ratio provides a measurement that allows the contributions made by each type of unit, job, or lot sold to be compared with each other.

Comparing gross profit on different models, units, jobs, or lots provides information to make decisions about product mix and pricing.

This analysis is also applicable when comparing remodeling jobs or analyzing profit performance of different development parcels. The greater the gross profit ratio, the higher the potential for net profits.

Two factors make a direct contribution to gross profits: sales price and cost of sales. Sales price is generally set by the local market, and often a builder, remodeler, or developer has little room to increase prices to improve the gross profit ratio without affecting the sales velocity (how many units can be sold in a given period of time). However, when the sales price is below market value, a builder, remodeler, or developer can increase the gross profit ratio by raising the sales price.

Reducing cost of sales (lot cost and direct cost) and, specifically, direct construction cost presents the greatest potential for increasing gross profit. Control

Model A

Sales price	$155,000
Cost of sales	− $108,500
Gross profit	= $46,500
Gross profit ratio	$46,500/155,000=30%

Example

	Model B	Model C	Model D	Total
Sales price	$174,500	$199,750	$215,000	
Cost of sales	$135,412	$147,416	$161,680	
Gross profit	$39,088	$52,334	$53,320	
Gross profit ratio	22.4%	26.2%	24.8%	
Units sold	5	2	3	10
Gross profit by model	$195,440	$104,668	$159,960	$460,068

A change in product mix will give different results:

	Model B	Model C	Model D	Total
Units sold	3	4	3	10
Gross profit by model	$117,264	$209,336	$159,960	$486,560

The change in product mix accounts for an increase in gross profit of $26,492.

of direct construction costs starts with efficient designs and accurate estimates. In addition, the level of standard specifications, selection of materials, construction methods, efficiency of operations, negotiating skills, and scheduling will have a significant impact on the cost. Therefore, budgeting adequately for construction cost is not enough; standardized processes and procedures need to be established and implemented to ensure the planned outcome.

Part of the job of a builder, remodeler, or developer is to maintain the projected gross profit margin. This task requires special and detailed attention. A well-organized job cost accounting system provides the structure to track the construction cost by unit of construction. An overview of job cost accounting is presented in Chapter 9.

A standard minimum gross profit ratio should be established to determine whether or not to proceed with the construction of any unit. During the planning stage, gross profit analysis should be used to estimate gross profit ratios to weed out jobs that will not meet the desired gross profit ratio. Units or jobs that do not meet the criteria should be rejected or reviewed to see if changes could be made to have the job produce the targeted gross profit.

If, at the planning stage, a job or unit will not produce the desired or targeted gross profit ratio, rest assured that when it is built it will still not produce the desired results. As a general rule, builders, remodelers, and developers tend to lose, not gain, profit margin during the actual construction period. To achieve profits, you need to plan for profits and then follow one of Lee Evans' most popular axioms: "Compel events to conform to the plan."

Depending on the operating policies of each company, gross profit ratios between 25 and 30 percent are usually attainable goals and allow for a reasonable net profit. Remodeling operations generally require a higher gross profit ratio because the unknown factors in a remodeling job are usually greater than they are in new construction, increasing the risk factor involved in the project. The same situation is true for land developers. Risk factors coupled with the length of the projects demand a higher gross profit ratio in the 50 percent range.

Cash Flow Analysis

The cash flow report is one of the most useful tools available to a builder, remodeler, or developer (Table 8–1). It identifies all cash sources and cash uses within a given period. It can be a historical statement as well as a planning tool. A historical cash flow report analyzes the inflows and outlays of cash in previous periods. The figures in the cash flow report must be integrated with the figures in the balance sheet and income statement of the same period. When used as a planning tool, this statement must take into account all potential sources and uses of cash.

The procedure to follow in preparing a projected cash flow report is relatively simple. The statement has the following major sections:

- Beginning cash balance
- Receipts (sources of cash)
- Disbursements (uses of cash)
- Cash requirements
- Ending cash balance

Beginning Cash Balance. The cash balance at the end of the previous period becomes the beginning cash balance.

Receipts (Sources of Cash). Analyze all possible cash sources based on past experience and on the company's general plan, objectives, and projected level of sales. Identify each source of cash as from home sales, remodeling, construction loan draws, land sales, sale of fixed assets, owners' contributions, or other loans. In other words, account for and classify by source all anticipated deposits to the cash account. The total of cash sources and beginning cash balance constitutes the total cash available for the period.

Disbursements (Uses of Cash). Cash uses are determined by the level of activity established for the business. Look carefully at the sales plan to determine when you need to repay construction loans. Review the construction schedule to determine payroll needs and approximate pay dates for suppliers and subcontractors. Generally, administrative expenses remain the same month after month

Table 8.1	Cash Flow Report For the Year ended December 31, 20XX		
Beginning cash balance			$100,000
Sources of cash:			
Sales		$11,330,000	
Collection on receivables		$8,000	
Collection on notes		$14,000	
Deposits by customers		$18,000	
Construction loan costs		$5,954,000	
Total cash receipts			$17,324,000
Total cash available			$17,424,000
Cash disbursements:			
Accounts payable		$7,973,600	
Payroll, net		$453,200	
Construction loan payments		$8,594,000	
Taxes			
Payroll		$54,900	
Real estate		$9,000	
Deposit on land purchase		$100,000	
Interest		$25,000	
Total disbursements			$17,209,700
Cash excess (or shortage)			$214,300
Cash requirements:			
Borrowed funds needed			
Repayment of borrowed funds			$100,000
Ending cash balance			**$114,300**

regardless of construction, remodeling, or land development activity. However, you must review the annual budget plan for this type of expense and make allowances for expenses that are not paid monthly, such as insurance premiums for vehicles, builder's risk, and Workers' Compensation.

Financing and marketing expenditures are generally related to the level of sales and construction activities. The timing of the expenses is critical to the cash flow. Classify cash outlays such as payroll taxes, deposits on estimated income tax, insurance premiums, and other expenses that are not paid monthly within the period they are due.

Examine decisions about land purchases, purchases of vehicles, construction and office equipment, and incorporate any projected cash outlays into the appropriate budget period.

Cash Requirements. The company must maintain a minimum cash balance to support its day-to-day business functions. To meet this minimum balance, companies occasionally borrow money from financial institutions in the form of a short-term loan or line of credit. The cash flow report should show the activity of the short-term loans or line of credit in the cash requirements section.

Ending Cash Balance. To determine the ending cash balance, deduct cash uses from cash available. When preparing a historical cash flow report, this amount must agree with the ending cash balance that appears on the balance sheet.

The primary historical use of the cash flow report is to evaluate a company's past performance and to plan for the future. For example, has the company followed plans and objectives? Should remedial action be taken if the ending cash balance is not adequate to carry the cash needs for the following period?

The projected cash flow analyzes future cash needs and evaluates availability of cash resources. This analysis provides you with timely information about cash needs and cash availability. Accurate cash flow forecasts allow a builder, developer, and remodeler to pre-arrange lines of credit for periods in which cash flow will be insufficient and to explore other potential cash sources.

Financial Ratio Analysis

A ratio is the relationship between two or more numbers. Financial ratios identify relationships among the different classifications in financial statements to measure financial strength, efficiency of operation, and return on investment, to name a few.

Ratios can be used as:

- Planning tools or standards by which to measure past performance
- Guidelines to evaluate the position of the business against industry standards
- A means to evaluate historical data and determine trends

Financial ratio analysis helps evaluate the company's present financial position, identify problems and areas that can be improved, and make decisions that will enhance profitability. The four major financial ratio categories measure liquidity, profitability, leverage, and return on investment.

Liquidity Ratios

Liquidity means solvency, the ability to convert assets to cash. Liquidity ratios evaluate a company's ability to meet its cash obligations, generally short term. These ratios are important to lenders because the ratios determine a borrower's ability to pay back debt. Monitor the company's liquidity ratio closely to ensure the company can stay in business and maintain its ability to borrow money. Measures of

liquidity are discussed below, using figures from the balance sheet shown in Table 8.1.

Current Ratio. This ratio is the most commonly used to measure liquidity or solvency. It measures the ability to pay current debts or liabilities with available current assets:

$$\frac{\text{Current Assets}}{\text{Current Liabilities}} = \frac{15{,}685{,}000}{9{,}200{,}000} = 1.7$$

Current assets include cash and all other assets that would be converted to cash during the normal course of operations within a fiscal or calendar year. Current liabilities are debts due to be paid on demand or within a fiscal or calendar year. The difference between current assets and current liabilities (current assets minus current liabilities) is commonly referred to as working capital.

$$\text{Current Assets} - \text{Current Liabilities} = \text{Working Capital}$$
$$\$15{,}685{,}000 - \$9{,}200{,}000 = \$6{,}485{,}000$$

Working capital consists of resources (current assets) that are available after you have paid all current obligations. Working capital measures the capabilities for business expansion and growth. When analyzed with other ratios, working capital also determines efficient use of company resources. In this analysis, a high liquidity ratio may be as detrimental as a low ratio because a high one indicates inadequate use of available resources. A ratio of 2 is desirable. However, 1.5 is a more typical current ratio in the homebuilding industry as a whole.

Acid Test Ratio. The acid test ratio is a refinement of the current ratio and is a stricter test of liquidity. Instead of including total current assets, this ratio uses only quick assets: cash or any other current asset that can be easily converted to cash, such as accounts receivables and short-term cash investments. The acid test ratio does not include inventories.

$$\frac{\text{Quick Assets}}{\text{Current Liabilities}} = \frac{\$985{,}000}{\$9{,}200{,}000} = 0.11$$

Throughout the industry, homebuilding, remodeling, and land development companies generally have a low acid test ratio. Generally, companies are heavily financed by lenders and the bulk of current assets is in inventory.

Profitability Ratios

Profitability ratios measure a company's profitability as determined by its net income. The net income of a business appears in the income statement. Therefore, profitability ratios represent relationships among the different categories in the income statement as they relate to sales or total revenues. The following profitability ratios contain figures taken from the income statement shown in Table 8–2:

Each one of these ratios provides a measurement of performance for each of the areas. Target ratios should be established for each area and actual ratios compared and analyzed against the targets.

You can determine other measures of profitability or efficient use of resources from the relationships between classifications from the income statement and the balance sheet.

Efficiency Ratios

The figures below are taken from the balance sheet shown in Table 8–1 and the income statement in Table 8–2.

Asset Turnover Ratio. This ratio measures how efficiently a business uses its resources.

$$\frac{Sales}{Assets} = \frac{\$29,650,000}{\$17,135,000} = 1.73$$

Inventory Turnover Ratio. Inventories amount to a large percentage of a builder's or developer's assets. (Generally, a remodeler is not as concerned with inventories because a remodeler works under contract without taking ownership of properties.) The inventory turnover ratio measures the movement of inventory during a given accounting period and allows the builder or developer to evaluate inventory levels. It also reflects the efficiency of the construction process and the length of the cycle time.

$$\frac{Sales}{Inventory} = \frac{\$29,650,000}{\$14,700,000} = 2.02$$

Table 8.2	**Income Statement**

Land ratio

$$\frac{Land}{Sales} = \frac{\$3,700,000}{\$29,650,000} = 12.5\%$$

Direct construction cost ratio

$$\frac{Direct\ Cost}{Sales} = \frac{\$17,150,000}{\$29,650,000} = 57.8\%$$

Cost of sales ratio

$$\frac{Cost\ of\ Sales}{Sales} = \frac{\$20,850,000}{\$29,650,000} = 70.3\%$$

Gross profit ratio

$$\frac{Gross\ Profit}{Sales} = \frac{\$8,800,000}{\$29,650,000} = 29.7\%$$

Indirect construction cost ratio

$$\frac{Indirect\ Cost}{Sales} = \frac{\$860,000}{\$29,650,000} = 2.9\%$$

Financing expense ratio

$$\frac{Financing\ expenses}{Sales} = \frac{\$1,560,000}{\$29,650,000} = 5.3\%$$

Sales & marketing expense ratio

$$\frac{Sales\ \&\ Marketing}{Sales} = \frac{\$2,200,000}{\$29,650,000} = 7.4\%$$

General & administrative (G&A) expense ratio

$$\frac{G\ \&\ A}{Sales} = \frac{\$1,425,000}{\$29,650,000} = 4.8\%$$

Total operating expense ratio

$$\frac{Total\ Expenses}{Sales} = \frac{\$6,045,000}{\$29,650,000} = 20.4\%$$

Net profit ratio

$$\frac{Net\ Profit}{Sales} = \frac{\$2,755,000}{\$29,650,000} = 9.3\%$$

Leverage Ratios

Leverage is a somewhat abstract term that measures how heavily the assets of a firm are financed by a lender versus owner resources. Lenders are interested in this ratio because the higher the leverage, the greater their risk. By the same token, the higher the leverage, the greater the return on investment if any profits are left after paying the interest on the debt. High leverage also increases the investor's risk. The following leverage ratios use figures from the balance sheet shown in Table 8–1.

Owners' Equity to Total Assets Ratio. This ratio shows what percentage of the assets are financed by owner investment versus borrowed funds:

$$\frac{\text{Owners' Equity}}{\text{Assets}} = \frac{\$3,635,000}{\$17,135,000} = 21\%$$

Ratio of Total Liabilities to Owners' Equity. The lower the ratio, the stronger the owners' position with respect to the assets of the business:

$$\frac{\text{Liabilities}}{\text{Owners' Equity}} = \frac{\$13,500,000}{\$3,635,000} = 3.71$$

Return on Investment Ratios

These ratios measure the return on investment when investment is defined as either the total resources of a business or the owners' investment. The figures below are taken from the balance sheet shown in Table 8–1 and the income statement in Table 8–2.

Return on Assets Ratio

$$\frac{\text{Net Profit}}{\text{Assets}} = \frac{\$2,755,000}{\$17,135,000} = 16\%$$

Return on Owners' Investment Ratio

$$\frac{\text{Net Profit}}{\text{Owners' Equity}} = \frac{\$2,755,000}{\$3,635,000} = 76\%$$

The ultimate goal of maximizing profits is to obtain the highest possible return on owners' investment or capital at risk. Obviously, the higher the risk, the higher the return you can hope to achieve. Conversely, for a lower risk, a lower return is accept-

able. Of course the higher the risk the higher the chance of no return or a negative return. In real life, builders, remodelers, and developers are in business to make high returns on safe projects. Exercise caution and carefully research the facts when faced with risks not easily or completely understood.

A variety of factors affect the return on owners' investment. By isolating some of those factors, you can take steps to improve the ratio. Return on investment is the product of net profit, efficient use of resources, and the degree of leverage. The following formula expresses these relationships:

Return on Investment = Return on Sales × Asset Turnover × Leverage

$$\frac{\text{Profits}}{\text{Equity}} = \frac{\text{Profits}}{\text{Sales}} \times \frac{\text{Sales}}{\text{Assets}} \times \frac{\text{Assets}}{\text{Equity}}$$

$$\frac{\$2755000}{\$3635000} = \frac{\$2755000}{\$29650000} \times \frac{\$29650000}{\$17135000} \times \frac{\$17135000}{\$3635000}$$

$$76\% = 9.3\% \times 1.73 \times 4.71$$

NAHB's *The Business of Building-Cost of Doing Business Study* provides ratios prevalent in the industry. The ratios are broken down by geographical areas and sales volume. This publication provides a good guideline or point of comparison between a company and the industry.

Ways to Improve Ratios

An improvement in any or all three components of the return on investment formula increases the return on invested capital. Control and planning are the key words to remember for improving return on invested capital.

Return on Sales

Control of Land Development and Direct Construction Costs. Each house or unit built, each remodeling job, and each lot developed must be a cost center, meaning all costs relating to a house or unit, remodeling job, or parcel are accumulated in an individual account. Within each cost center, costs must be broken down into subcategories or cost codes. Each cost code represents a point of control to determine if the actual costs are coming in as estimated. Use the same cost codes used in preparing accurate estimates prior to start of construction to accumulate actual costs. Periodically compare the actual and estimated costs to make sure actual costs are under control. Give special attention to variances and change orders.

Control of Indirect Construction Cost. Efficient job management helps control indirect construction cost. Because costs are time driven, keeping to schedules is critical to controlling this category of cost.

Control of Operating Expenses. You need to budget carefully for these expenses, take steps to ensure that plans are followed, and balance fixed expenses with sales and production volume. Fixed expenses can become a burden if volume or sales revenues decrease, whereas variable expenses tend to decrease proportionately with decreases in volume. A business that minimizes fixed expenses has greater flexibility to withstand the lows of the economic cycle. Fixed expenses that are balanced with sales and construction volume are crucial to the success of homebuilding, remodeling, and development firms.

Like indirect construction cost, most operating expenses are time driven. Standardized systems and procedures help control these types of costs and expenses because standardization directly increases efficiency of the work force.

Asset Turnover

The asset turnover ratio measures the efficient use of resources. The level of activity planned for the company should determine the amount of resources needed.

Plan the Sales Volume. This step requires considerable involvement by builders, remodelers, or developers and their sales managers. Two variables come into play when planning or projecting sales volume: the economic conditions of the marketplace and the company's resources.

Study the marketplace by looking at general economic conditions and local economic conditions and market trends, as well as forecasts made by government agencies and trade associations.

When analyzing the company's resources, consider the goals and objectives of the business, the services provided, products, available resources, growth potential, additional sources of funds, and management capabilities.

After analyzing the economic factors and the company's resources, a meaningful sales plan can be developed. This plan should take into account types of products and services, product mix, pricing policies, and time line. You can then plan availability of assets to sustain the production level in terms of land, construction materials, human resources, and inventories.

Leverage

The ratio of assets to owners' equity, known as leverage, can be a trade-off depending on economic conditions. Generally, the trade off for an increase in leverage can be a decrease in return on sales because the increase in borrowed funds increases interest expenses. At the same time the additional capital can generate more sales with the same capital investment by the owners, thus potentially increasing the return.

An increase in interest rates may have a dramatic effect on a business with high leverage. Exercise caution in this situation because high interest expense may absorb all additional profits or even create a negative return.

Breakeven Analysis

Breakeven analysis is another analytical tool available to builders, remodelers, and developers. In essence, breakeven analysis attempts to determine the sales volume required to cover all costs and expenses of the company. Breakeven analysis can be a quick and easy way to determine minimum sales volumes. It will calculate how many units, jobs, or lots need to close in a given period to break even (no profit or loss).

To calculate the breakeven point, cost and expenses need to be classified into either (a) variable cost and expenses or (b) fixed cost and expenses. Chapter 3 discusses the nature of fixed and variable costs and expenses.

The next step is to calculate the contribution margin. Contribution margin is the difference between sales and variable costs or the margin left to cover fixed expenses. For example:

Unit Sales Price − Variable Costs and Expenses = Contribution Margin

To calculate the breakeven point, divide the contribution margin into the fixed cost. The result will be the number of units, jobs, or lots needed to sell to reach the breakeven point.

For example:

Sales price/unit	$100,000
Variable cost and expenses/unit	$75,000
Total Fixed cost	$500,000

To calculate the contribution margin:

Sales price	$100,000
Variable cost and expenses	$75,000
Contribution margin	$25,000

To calculate breakeven:

$$\frac{\text{Fixed cost}}{\text{Contribution margin}} = \frac{\$500,000}{25,000} = 20 \text{ units or houses}$$

Or 20 units @ $100,000 = $2,000,000

By making a small adjustment to the formula, you can calculate the breakeven in dollar volume. This approach will be more useful when dealing with a diverse product line. The breakeven point is calculated by using the contribution margin ratio.

Example

To calculate contribution margin ratio:

$$\frac{\text{Contribution Margin}}{\text{Sales Price}} = \frac{\$25,000}{\$100,000} = .25$$

To calculate breakeven:

$$\frac{\text{Fixed Cost}}{\text{Contribution Margin Ratio}} = \frac{\$500,000}{.25} = \$2,000,000$$

The objective of the breakeven analysis is to establish the sales volume needed to cover the fixed expenses and begin to make profits. If the sales volume as calculated in the breakeven analysis is not realistic, there are two other options: improve the contribution margin and/or reduce fixed costs and expenses.

CHAPTER 9

Overview of Job Cost Accounting

As discussed earlier in this book, the general accounting system accumulates all construction costs in a single account: direct construction cost. The general accounting system does not allocate costs to individual units, remodeling jobs, or land parcels; therefore, this system does not identify the cost per unit, job, or land parcel.

The job cost accounting system is a subsystem or subsidiary of the general accounting system. The bookkeeper accumulates construction costs on a unit-by-unit, job-by-job, or project-by-project basis in the job cost subsidiary. The total of all jobs in the job cost subsidiary must equal the balance in the direct construction cost account of the general ledger.

The job cost subsidiary provides information for builders, remodelers, and developers to manage, control costs, monitor operations, and make sound business decisions. The level of detail incorporated into the job cost system determines the type and quality of management reports the system can generate.

Designing the System

In the job cost subsidiary, the cost of each unit of production is accumulated in a separate account. In addition, the different types of costs are identified by cost codes in each account. Because the cost codes form the basis of the job cost system and become control points, they need to be selected carefully. Each purchasing unit and/or work unit must have a separate cost code and the order of the cost code must follow the construction sequence. Most importantly, cost codes used to accumulate actual cost must be the same cost codes used when estimating the jobs.

When designing the job cost system, consider the following guidelines because the job cost codes must reflect the way each company builds, remodels, or develops land and the nature of the products and services involved.

- Different geographical areas have different building requirements (such as type of foundation).
- The use of labor may vary. (Some companies use their own crews and others subcontract.)
- Purchasing units may be more specialized in large metropolitan areas.
- The type of product or service varies from company to company (detached versus attached housing, additions versus bathroom, upgrades, planned unit developments versus small parcels).

The job cost accounting system must be integrated with estimating and purchasing. To ensure comparison of estimates with actual cost, the cost codes used to accumulate actual cost must be the same as the cost codes used to estimate the jobs. In addition, it is highly recommended that the cost codes follow the construction, remodeling, or development sequence. Cost codes accounts can then be closed as construction progresses, thereby reducing the number of items that a builder, remodeler, or developer must analyze at any particular time. This will also provide the structure to integrate the invoice approval process into the scheduling function.

To streamline the analytical process, the job cost accounting system could classify cost codes into con-

struction and development phases. For example, the *preliminary phase* will include all costs incurred prior to start of construction, such as architectural and engineering fees and permits. The *preparation phase* will includes cost codes associated with site clearing, excavation, and foundation. Depending on the construction methods and requirements of each company, there could be from 3 to 10 construction phases with 5 to 25 cost codes per phase.

Developers generally do not require as many cost codes to accumulate the development costs. Therefore, segregating the cost codes into phases might not be necessary other than to segregate the planning phase from the construction phase. For remodelers, the type of remodeling work will determine the need for segregating cost codes into phases. For example, phases might not be necessary for a remodeler that mainly redoes kitchens and baths. In other instances, however, in which the remodeling work involves room additions and whole-house remodeling, grouping cost codes by phases might prove helpful. The purpose of the phases is to concentrate attention on a smaller number of cost codes as the work progresses.

Appendix E presents a chart of accounts of job cost codes. When applying the suggested list of cost codes to your business, use only the cost code that represents a purchasing unit or work order. Unnecessary detail will hamper the system and produce worthless information that will detract from critical issues.

For example, when a subcontractor supplies labor and materials, having a cost code for labor and a cost code for materials is not necessary. In fact, having two cost codes creates unnecessary work because the two cost codes will have to be added together to compare with the negotiated contract price, which in this case is the control point. Now, if materials are purchase directly and only the labor is part of the subcontract agreement, there should be two cost codes to control not only the labor cost but also the cost of materials purchased.

If a company is issuing purchase orders, there should be a cost code for each purchase order. For example, if gravel, sand, and concrete block are ordered at the same time from the same supplier, there should be only one cost code to accumulate the cost of all three items. If , conversely, gravel and sand are ordered from a different supplier, there should be two cost codes—one for sand and gravel and one for concrete blocks. Never break down an invoice into two or more cost codes. Doing so becomes time-consuming and increases the chance of entering the cost in the wrong account.

The total amount of dollars spent on one material is irrelevant at this point in time. The object is to control the purchasing units estimated prior to the start of construction, remodeling, or development. If the invoice does not match the estimate, any discrepancies or variances are caught immediately.

Use the job cost chart of accounts in Appendix E as a guideline or checklist to set up a job cost chart of accounts that will suit your needs. A good objective for homebuilding is to have between 75 and 100 cost codes. More than 100 will begin to clutter the system and hinder efficient processing of the accounting data.

Code the Invoices

Proper coding of invoices is essential to any job cost accounting system. Cost reports are useless unless the data presented is reliable and accurate. Assigning an account number to each invoice is generally the weak link in a job cost accounting system. By the time invoices arrive, employees may not remember why the materials were purchased nor where they were used. Answering these questions becomes a guessing game. Moreover, invoices are occasionally lost, misplaced, or damaged while they are being coded.

Establish a system that is going to facilitate the coding process and ensure the reliability of the accounting data. A purchase order system provides the best solution to the coding problem because purchase orders are coded when the materials are ordered or the labor scheduled. However, if a purchase order system is not in place, when ordering, give suppliers the materials cost code number as the

purchase order number. The cost code will then appear in the invoice under purchase order number. Keep in mind that the invoice should also make reference as to the job where the materials were delivered or the work done.

Improve Control With A Purchase Order System

A purchase order system provides the following advantages. Improvement in any of these areas will increase cost control and potentially increase profits:

- Confirms a verbal or telephone purchase
- Confirms anticipated delivery dates
- Fixes prices on will-call orders
- Provides written reference of purchase
- Gives the superintendent a reference or control point to check quantity and quality of materials delivered
- Serves as proof of delivery and authorization for payment
- Facilitates job cost posting and accounting
- Allows the builder, remodeler, or developer to delegate much of the purchasing function to nonmanagers
- Provides a reference to quoted prices
- Gives current information on outstanding obligations

Preparing Job Cost Reports

The reports generated by the job cost system must be timely, standardized, and must include the following information for each unit or remodeling job under construction or project being developed:

- Budget and actual costs
- Variances or differences between budget and actual costs
- Committed cost or outstanding purchase orders

Make sure each cost code represents a point of control. The job cost reports should highlight variance information. Interesting details with no impact on cost control issues are useless. The overall objective of the job cost control system is to produce accurate cost information that builders, remodelers, and developers can use to increase the profitability of their businesses.

Too frequently, too many reports and an overabundance of detail overshadows the key information that builders, remodelers, and developers need. In large companies, top managers do not need reports with as much detail as lower level managers. Detailed reports can be made available to top managers on request.

CHAPTER 10

Processing Systems

Accounting involves processing large quantities of data to prepare financial and management reports necessary for the operation and management of a business.

In-house Computers

Owning a computer is now a reality for most builders because the price of personal computers has become affordable and the number of software packages available for homebuilding, remodeling, and land development businesses has increased. Many builders, developers, and remodelers believe that the best processing system is an in-house computer system because it enables them to enter data and generate reports whenever needed.

Manual Systems

A manual accounting system can be effective and can produce the same quality of output as any computer system, but a manual system is labor intensive, time-consuming, and prone to human error because numbers and information must be copied and transferred to many different ledgers. Today, manual systems are nearly obsolete. Even the very small-volume business can computerize its accounting functions. Many accounting packages are user-friendly and have been designed for nonaccountants who handle many of the accounting duties behind the scenes. But beware: Errors in data entry are not uncommon and will affect any computer system.

Even though a manual system may be cost effective for some small-volume businesses, the options available in accounting software and the ease of using a computer system make a computerized accounting process far more attractive than a manual one. Computerized systems also offer speedy processing and the capability to produce more timely reports. Remember, though, that the integrity of the information and the usefulness of the reports that come from the accounting system are dependent on the accuracy of the data entry and the accounts used to classify the data. This holds true for either a manual or a computer system. Follow the NAHB Chart of Accounts to obtain the best possible output from the accounting system.

One-Write Systems

A One-Write or pegboard system is a manual system that uses time-saving devices to record accounting data. Prelined forms, carbon strips, and pressure-sensitive carbons (or no-carbon-required paper) allow a check to be written and posted to multiple journals, ledgers, and job cost records in one step. This type of system was very popular prior to the advent of the personal computer. It offered small-volume builders, remodelers, and developers a way to improve their own manual systems and get better organized if they were not ready to computerize.

Computerizing Your Accounting Function

When computerizing the accounting function be aware of the myth that computers solve all problems of processing accounting data and provide timely and accurate reports. The old axiom, "garbage in, garbage out," still holds true.

If you are still using a manual system, before you purchase a computer system you should have an efficient and disciplined financial reporting system and plan in place. Set up procedures to enter, process, and store or file information; update files; and design reports you can prepare whether you process accounting data manually or with a computer. Well-documented manual procedures and controls with clearly identified reporting requirements are essential for a smooth transition to a computerized accounting system.

When implementing a change, be it from a manual system to a computer system or from one computer system to another, allow more time for processing than under the old system because learning to use any new system will at first take some time. Some systems are easier than others to implement and do not take much time to learn, but remember that people learn at different speeds. In many instances it takes a good amount of perseverance to undergo the implementation of any new system. Many failures occur at this stage because the builder, remodeler, or developer lacks the commitment and decisiveness necessary to endure the implementation process. Once the implementation is completed it is generally smooth sailing, especially with the smaller systems.

Accounting Applications

Builders, remodelers, and developers tend to be happy with an integrated computerized accounting system—one that can post the data to the general and subsidiary ledgers and also interact with the management reporting functions, including budgeting, estimating, purchasing, scheduling, cost control, and other record-intensive activities. Even if you are starting by computerizing just the accounting function, look at software that has the capabilities to integrate other functionalities into the system so that you will have the capacity available when you are ready for it.

When shopping for a computer, be sure to purchase hardware that:

- Has the capabilities and is compatible with the accounting software you need and other software applications you may anticipate needing.
- Provides reliability and outstanding support service from the vendor. Computer down time (when the computer is out of service) can prove extremely costly.
- Includes a strong support package from the vendor for the crucial installation phase and an 800 telephone number for telephone troubleshooting during the life of the hardware. When called upon, service representatives should be able to make recommendations for enhancements and improvements to the system.
- Has enough disk storage space and random access memory (RAM) to run your software efficiently.
- Is as powerful as you can afford because whatever you buy will likely be obsolete in 2 years because development of new technology is so rapid.

To be sure that you purchase a computer system that matches your needs, attend NAHB-sponsored seminars and workshops on computer software at the NAHB Convention and other meetings. If necessary, seek the advice of a professional computer consultant.

You need to look for user-friendly, integrated accounting and cost control packages that meet your requirements and reporting needs. As you look at software, ask vendors how long they have been in business and how many users are presently on the system. Also ask for a list of builders, remodelers, or developers who have purchased the package and who can offer an opinion. Make sure to call several users, and if possible visit the user's site that most closely resembles your type of operation.

An automated accounting system puts data into a database. This database generally can be stored in either of two locations, locally or remotely.

Local databases contain information collected as part of the accounting process. The information is then input onto the hard drive of the computer running the accounting software. One software package, with one database running on a single computer, is an example of a local database. This is designed for one user at a time accessing the information.

Another way that data is stored locally is on a server (sometimes referred to as a file or database server). Computers are then connected to the server using a hub. The only difference is that server-based software can handle more than one user at a time accessing the same information. People choose to use file servers for several reasons:

- Better access to the information
- Better performance of the system
- Easier maintenance of the software
- Ease of backing up the data

The way your organization is structured will help you determine whether you need remote access to your data. People in different locations needing immediate access to accounting data is the biggest reason to have a central database with remote access (sometimes called a WAN, or wide area network). When data is stored remotely it requires some sort of communication lines to transmit the information. Typically this requires a higher level of technical staffing at both the central and remote location.

Because the cost of the communication lines and technical staff can be significant, larger builders have used wide area networks more often than have smaller builders. However, the Internet gives the small builder the same capabilities as a wide area network. Software systems that run on the Internet are also called ASP (application service provider) or Web-based systems. This means the software and data are stored on a server (just like the local example above), except the server is not in the builder's office connected by a hub. Both the software and the data are on the Internet. All the builder needs is an Internet connection.

An ASP system reduces the investment that a builder makes in hardware, software maintenance, and technical staff and provides the ability to access company data from any authorized Internet connection. Your information is available to you 24/7, and there are no "special" requirements. Large and small builders alike will benefit from Internet-ready software. Make sure you stay abreast of new developments and changes in the computer and software arena, as this area remains in constant change.

Service Bureaus

Service bureaus are independent organizations that process data for clients. As prices of computers and computer software declined, service bureaus lost most of their appeal to builders, remodelers, and developers, who now feel more comfortable with an in-house system. However, service bureaus still provide a diversity of options that can be appealing. For example, preparing payroll with the numerous reports required by different government groups can be time-consuming and distracting when done in-house. This activity is easily delegated to the service bureau to (a) free the bookkeeper to spend more time on cost reports and analysis and (b) control confidentiality of information. Thus, the service bureau remains a viable option for the small-volume builder, developer, and remodeler for specific tasks.

Other Applications

The versatility of today's computers and the availability of software lets builders, developers, and remodelers explore the many practical and efficient applications of the computer.

Popular software other than accounting software can be grouped into four main categories:

- Word processing and desktop publishing programs
- Spreadsheets or electronic sheets
- Database management programs
- Drawing and computer-aided design (CAD) programs

Each group has numerous programs with many features and levels of sophistication, and Windows technology has made these programs more user friendly.

Word processing systems save time and provide an unmatched professional appearance. They allow you to store and quickly prepare (as you need them) such frequently used documents as form letters, contract formats, and standard notices. Spreadsheets are great analytical and planning tools. They make management reports easy to prepare because they can perform mathematical functions. They also allow a builder, remodeler, or developer to change scenarios or variables for a quick recalculation of a projected outcome.

Versatile database management programs store and sort statistical information; maintain mailing lists; collect and analyze sales and production data; track personnel, clients, prospects, and others.

CAD programs are increasingly popular among building, remodeling, and development firms. CAD programs can serve as a sales tool because they provide the capability of making architectural changes on a computer screen and allow a builder or remodeler to alter plans quickly and at a minimal cost. Developers can use CAD for creating site plans. Currently, through the use of a special set of attributes most CAD programs can produce "intelligent plans" that show material applications on the set of plans as well as provide material takeoffs.

Computer technology constantly changes. Therefore, you must stay current with new hardware and software applications. Computers are affordable and critical tools in the management of a building, remodeling, or land development firm. If you are not using a computer now, you should begin the research and education process to incorporate the use of computers into your daily operations. If you are already using a computer, you should find out if you are taking full advantage of its capabilities and keep abreast of new upgrades and developments that will further enhance your applications.

CHAPTER 11

Tips for Multiproject Companies

When a firm works on more than one project at a time, an individual project operates almost like a mini-company within the main company.

A builder, remodeler, or developer should identify the contribution each project makes to the overall profitability of the company and evaluate each project on its own merit. A key part of increasing profitability is to identify problems as soon as possible. Measuring the performance of a multiproject firm on a project-by-project basis helps isolate problems. A builder would further evaluate performance by model, a remodeler by the type of job, and a developer by the type of lot. However, this discussion will focus primarily on the project level.

General Accounting

A multiproject company uses the same accounting structure as a single-project company. Sales for each project or subdivision need to be recorded at the subdivision level, as well as all cost and expenses associated with the sale. Most accounting software provides the structure to record the activity for each subdivision or project by itself and is also able to aggregate the activity of all projects to report the activity of the company as a whole. Some programs refer to this capability as being able to tract revenues and expenses by division or departments.

When a builder has different types of housing units in a subdivision (for example, single family, patio homes, and townhouses), separate revenue and cost of sales accounts should be set up to tract the different product lines.

Chart of Accounts

A multiproject company uses the same NAHB Chart of Accounts as a single-project company because the accounts are the same for both. As the company grows there might be a need to separate certain types of expenditures. For example, a small company would have a telephone expense account in which to record expenses for its office and mobile telephones, radios, and beepers. Accumulating all communications expenses in one account might be sufficient in a small company because the owner or top manager usually has direct control of all communication devices. As the company grows and new employees are added, the company will use more mobile phones, radios, and beepers; to exercise better control over the expenditures, separate expense accounts will be set up for office phones, mobile phones, radios, and beepers.

Expansion of the chart of accounts is triggered not so much by multiple projects but by an increase in the number of employees and an increased need for control as the firm expands and its owners and top managers find themselves removed from the day-to-day operations.

Each project or subdivision must use the same structure or chart of accounts to accumulate sales revenue and cost of sales. Most accounting software provides the capability of keeping financial data by department, division, or project. When the bookkeeper enters the revenues and expenses, the software will ask for the department, division, or project number, and it will automatically store the information by department, division, or project.

Each project must be evaluated on its own merits because each project must contribute to the overall profitability of the operation. Gross profit margin analysis is paramount at the project level. (See Chapter 8.)

The accounting system should be able to identify problems as soon as possible. The profitability of each project can be measured by accumulating revenues by project and matching cost of sales and expenses directly to the project revenues. By segmenting the data, you can easily identify problem areas by project.

Profit Centers

Classifying revenues, cost of sales, and direct project expenses on a project-by-project basis creates separate profit centers. Each project must have its own separate budget with its projected profit to compare actual results with the planned performance. The comparison enhances the evaluation of each project and makes it easier to identify cost control problems. Establishing each project as a separate profit center is the first step in maximizing profitability.

In addition, the results of each project will also provide a measurement of the performance of the manager in charge of the project. Depending on the size of the organization and the number and size of the projects, one employee could be responsible for more than one project.

Job Costing

For a multiproject company, job costing is no different than it is for a single-project company. Job costs should still be estimated on a house-per-house basis and the actual cost accumulated in Account 1430, direct construction costs. Follow the same procedures and use the same reports to control costs as outlined in Chapter 9.

The numbering system to identify units of construction is the only element that might need adjustment. Use block and lot number as previously discussed, and add project numbers to identify each unit for job costing. For example, the house under construction on block 4, lot 23, in project 12 would be known as unit 120423. The first two digits identify the project; the second two digits, the block; and the third two digits, the lot.

A numbering system that clearly identifies projects allows for easy grouping of cost reports by project, to summarize results, and to distribute reports to the managers responsible for the construction of each project.

Indirect Construction Cost

As discussed in Chapter 2, indirect construction costs are those costs that are necessary for the construction process but cannot be directly identified with a particular unit. Some examples of indirect construction costs are supervisory cost and cost of construction vehicles, temporary utilities, and construction offices.

Although many of these costs are indirect (not directly tied to a production unit), they are direct costs for the project and, as such, should be accounted for as part of the project. The manager responsible for the project would also be responsible for the indirect construction costs that are directly related to the project. Allocation of indirect construction costs to each project is necessary to determine the project's profitability and to evaluate the project manager's performance.

In the instances where the estimating, purchasing, and design functions are done in a central location, these costs are indirect to the project and should be accounted for as a cost to the company. You can allocate the total indirect cost for each project to the units built in each project by following any or all of the methods described in Chapter 7.

Marketing and Financing Expenses

Allocate to each project the marketing and financing expenses directly related to the project to determine the contribution each project makes to overall operating expenses and profit. The contribution margin generated by each project is calculated by deducting from the revenues the cost of sales and all indirect costs and expenses directly related to the project. The contribution margin is a true measurement of the performance of the project and the contribution the project makes to cover the general company overhead and profits.

General and Administrative Expenses

General and administrative expenses normally cannot be directly allocated to individual projects because they relate to the company as a whole. Because project managers have little or no control over these expenditures, do not allocate these expenses to the projects.

Financial Analysis

Prepare an income statement for each project; calculate gross profit and profitability ratios (as described in Chapter 8); make comparisons between projects, time periods, and projected results; and establish trends for projects by comparing previous ratios with present ratios.

In addition to the income statements by project, prepare an overall income statement for the company that includes all of the company's revenue-generating activities and analyze it by following the guidelines outlined in Chapter 8.

CHAPTER 12

Tips for Developers

Some members of the light construction industry only develop land, and some single-family builders diversify into land development as their companies grow. Although many similarities exist between homebuilding and land development, some factors pertaining only to land development merit consideration.

- The initial capital investment required for land development is generally larger and of longer duration than the capital investment required for homebuilding because of financing equity requirements.
- As a result of the long time frame from the initial land acquisition and negotiation phase through the approval process and completion of the development project, the risk factor is usually higher than it is for homebuilding.
- Land development projects are subject to lengthy approval processes requiring numerous local, state, and federal government approvals.
- Homeowners in neighboring subdivisions could have an impact on the design and specifications of the land plan.
- The planning and design is quite technical in nature and requires the involvement of highly trained engineers, land planners, and specialists in sensitive environmental issues.

- Supervision of the land development process is different from the supervision required during the homebuilding process. It requires a lot of testing and shooting of grades and elevations.
- Two elements to successful completion of a land development project are market analysis and feasibility studies.

General Accounting

The principles of general accounting, internal control, and financial analysis presented in this publication are applicable to land development companies as well as to companies that diversify into different construction activities, including land development. When performing more than one economic activity (homebuilding, land development, remodeling), each activity needs to be accounted for as a separate cost/profit center to be able to evaluate the performance of each one. Otherwise it will be difficult to determine how much each activity contributed to the overall profitability of the company. The process and procedures for recording accounting information do not change. The NAHB Chart of Accounts presented in Appendix A sets up the structure to allow for the separate accountability of land development activities. The general accounting procedures for a developer are basically no different from those for a home builder.

The recognition of revenues for a land development operation follows the same guidelines as the recognition of income for a homebuilding business. Land development businesses recognize revenues at the time the title of the land transfers from the land development company to a bona fide purchaser. The purchaser can be an unrelated party or a subsidiary company that will build homes on the finished lots.

For internal control, developers (or builders diversifying into development) must follow the same rules of separation of duties, proper accountability, and the need to standardize practices and procedures presented in Chapter 6. The guidelines for cash management presented in Chapter 8 are universal in nature and therefore applicable to land development companies. Developers also need to coordinate their

accounting systems with their estimating and purchasing systems. The time line of development projects is particularly critical to optimize the overall success of the project.

The financial statements for a land development company will follow the same format as the statements for a homebuilding company, and the financial analysis of the financial statements will be done in a similar way using lots or parcels instead of units. Chapter 8 covers a number of financial ratios that help in the evaluation of a company's performance. Land development companies use the same ratio analysis that this book recommends for builders and remodelers. However, if a company is involved in both land development and homebuilding, the owner must make sure to account for each activity independently of the others so that he or she can measure the profitability of each activity.

The land development operations of a homebuilding company (or the building operations of a land development company) should be treated as a separate profit center. In other words, account for the land development revenues, costs, and expenses as if the development operation were an independent company that transfers the finished lots to the building operation or company at market value instead of at cost. By making the land development activities a separate profit center, you can evaluate the profitability of this activity and clearly identify whether problems in the profit equation result from land development or from homebuilding.

Chart of Accounts

The general NAHB Chart of Accounts presented in Appendix A is suitable for a land development company. In the asset section, Account 1410, land and land development cost, accumulates (a) the acquisition costs of undeveloped tracts of land and (b) the development costs to convert the tracts of land into developed or finished lots. On the liability side, Account 2220 is used to record the development and construction loans payable. If you want to isolate the development loans from the construction loans, you can easily establish a separate account for that purpose. For example, you can record land development loans in Account 2220, development loans payable, and construction loans in Account 2230, construction loans payable.

In the revenue and cost of sales section of the NAHB Chart of Accounts you will find separate accounts to record sales and cost of sales of undeveloped tracts of land. Sales of developed lots also go into a separate revenue account, as does the lot cost. By recording revenue and cost of sales of different activities into separate accounts, each activity is measured separately, allowing for evaluation of the contribution each activity makes to the overall profitability of the company.

Job Costing

Account 1410 accumulates all costs relating to the acquisition and development of raw land. This account offers no details on the types of costs nor on the parcel of land to which they relate. As with control of direct construction costs in the homebuilding operation, control of these costs in land development is critical to achieve superior profits. Thus, a subsidiary system similar to the job cost system working behind Account 1430 is required. Appendix F presents a list of accounts to be used in the land development job cost subsidiary.

As with homebuilding costs, keep the costs for each parcel of land or each development project separate. Separating the cost per development project allows the developer to evaluate each project by itself and simultaneously establish the cost base for distributing the development costs to the finished lots in each project. Each parcel of land is different, and site costs could vary significantly depending on site conditions (for example, wooded versus cleared, wetlands versus dry acreage, soil conditions and public utilities versus onsite drainage issues). Chapter 9 describes the use of the job cost subsidiary behind Account 1410.

Development Cost

Developers normally break down a development project into multiple phases. As lots are sold, additional phases are developed. It is advisable to have a separate budget for each phase and to collect the actual costs per phase to compare with the budget and ensure that development costs stay within the overall cost estimates.

The cost of developing the first phase of a project may be disproportionately higher than the cost of developing additional phases. Local jurisdictions often collect fees and exactions (such as impact fees, recreation fees, contributed acreage) for an entire development during the first phase of a multiphase project. In addition, entrance signs, initial utility runs to the site, amenities, and common-area landscaping often add to the costs at the start of a project. Because all completed lots must share a portion of the start-up, common-area, and amenities costs, cost allocations need to be based on the projected total cost of the project. Therefore, accuracy in planning and estimating is as crucial as the control of actual costs. Otherwise, if the costs get out of control toward the end of the project the last lots will have to absorb the cost overruns.

When developing more than one subdivision at the same time, each subdivision must be treated as a separate profit center. The accounting guidelines are similar to those applicable to home builders with multiple projects. (Chapter 11 includes a detailed discussion of how to handle cost control and accounting procedures if you have more than one project in process.)

Indirect Costs

Indirect costs are the necessary production costs not directly associated with the finished product. These costs are sometimes intangible in nature as opposed to the tangible costs for water and sewer pipes, curbs and gutters, and pools and other amenities included in land development plans. Examples of indirect costs are supervision, construction trailers, field office expenses, temporary utilities, and the like. In a land development operation, indirect costs are indirect to the lots but generally direct to the project, and you must add them to the development cost to determine the total cost to allocate to the developed lots.

Financing Costs

The costs of financing development projects are considered to be part of the cost of the project. As such, financing costs cannot be written off in the period in which they are incurred. Instead, they become part of the total cost of the project and are included in the cost of each individual lot through the allocation process.

Lot Cost Allocation

Because of the length of the development process and the practice of doing development work in phases, the lot cost allocation troubles some developers. However, various options are available.

If the tract of land is developed all at once, the allocation becomes easy. Divide the total cost of acquisition and development by the number of finished or developed lots. This method works under the assumption that the cost to develop each lot in the tract is the same. Of course, the profit margin for the higher-priced lots (wooded or lake front views) will be higher than the profit margin for the less-desirable or lower-priced lots. Some developers believe that the higher-priced lots should carry a higher percentage of the cost because on many occasions building on these lots will be more expensive. For example, the houses may have walk-out basements and so on.

Developers who follow this school of thought take a market approach to lot cost allocation. When using this method, determine the percentage of the total market value that is represented by the market value of each lot. For example, imagine a small parcel developed into five lots. The market value of each lot and the percentage of the total market value represented by each lot follows:

Lot Number	Market Value	Percentage of Total
1	$25,000	21%
2	$28,000	24%
3	$21,000	19%
4	$18,000	15%

The developer will allocate the total cost of the land development, $60,000, to each lot based on the percentage of total market value of the development that the market value of each lot represents:

Lot Number	Calculation	Development Cost
1	21% of $60,000	$12,600
2	24% of $60,000	$14,400
3	19% of $60,000	$11,400
4	15% of $60,000	$9,000
5	21% of $60,000	$12,600
		$60,000

When using this method, each lot will show the same gross profit ratio because the costs are distributed to each lot in proportion to its value. (See Chapter 8 for a discussion of gross profit.)

In a multiphase development, the initial phase or phases include costs that all lots in the project must share. Examples of such costs are costs associated with the zoning process, heavy front-end utility installations, offsite improvements required by local jurisdictions, and the cost of amenities. As phases are completed and lots are put on the market for sale or into housing production, you can allocate these costs to the developed lots in two ways:

- You can use a total estimated development cost and then divide by the total number of lots to be developed to determine unit cost, or use the market approach method described above. Periodically, you need to revise the total estimated development cost to include any variances incurred in all phases, including the new phase, and change the allocation to each lot from that point forward to reflect any changes or discrepancies with the earlier estimate.
- You can isolate the common-area costs from the costs of each phase. Using this method, you would use two numbers to allocate costs to each lot, one for a portion of the common costs and one for a portion of the development cost for the phase. Developers may want to use this method when there are great variations in the layout of the land that would cause significant variations

in development costs per phase and also significant market value variations between phases.

Lot Pricing

Lot pricing should always respond to market forces. Whether the lots are being sold to an unrelated party or put into production is immaterial; the pricing should be the same to avoid distorting the profit margins of the homebuilding process because of a lower-than-market cost basis for the developed lots. Owners and top managers need to evaluate the profitability of each segment of the company fairly. Therefore, profit margins for the homebuilding operations should not include development profits.

Financial Analysis

Chapter 8 discusses a number of tools, tests, and ratios that can be used to evaluate the financial results of a homebuilding company. All of the material discussed in this chapter can be used as well to evaluate the financial performance of a development company or operation.

CHAPTER 13

Tips for Remodelers

Remodelers typically function as general contractors and do not have to carry inventories nor construction financing during the building process. They are under contract to improve the customers' property, and the customer usually finances the construction cost. As a general contractor, the remodeler sometimes has to post a performance bond for the amount of the remodeling contract. Home builders typically do not have to post such bonds.

Many single-family builders diversify into remodeling when economic slumps cause potential move-up buyers to remodel their existing homes instead of buying a new home. Some companies work exclusively in remodeling and others, whose main operation is remodeling, diversify into single-family new construction, mostly custom homes.

No matter which combination of activities a company performs, anyone who makes remodeling a part of his or her business must recognize that remodeling is a different type of operation from new construction and requires separate accountability.

General Accounting

This chapter applies the principles of general accounting, internal control, and financial analysis to a remodeling company. Builders who diversify into different construction activities such as remodeling must identify and account for each activity separately. The process and procedures of recording the accounting information do not change. The NAHB Chart of Accounts sets up the structure to account for remodeling activities separately from homebuilding or development activities.

Recognizing income in a remodeling operation could be different from the recognition of income in new construction. The nature and size of the remodeling jobs and the size of the company typically will influence how to recognize it. Usually a remodeler works under contract; therefore, a work in process inventory account is not necessary. The company recognizes revenue as it bills out the job, and it recognizes cost of sales as invoices are received. However, remodelers still must maintain control over the remodeling costs by (a) comparing estimated and actual cost and (b) preparing a variance analysis report on each job. Accounting for and controlling costs will ensure achieving superior profit. Speculative remodeling jobs on houses bought by the company to fix up and resell should be accounted for as a separate type of activity or profit center.

The rules for internal control presented in Chapter 6 apply to any remodeling operation, including separation of crucial financial duties, proper accountability of funds, and standardization of practices and procedures. Cash management guidelines are universal in nature as is the need to coordinate the accounting system with the estimating and purchasing functions.

A remodeling company should follow the same format for financial statements and financial analysis as those for a homebuilding company. Chapter 8 covers a number of financial ratios that help a builder, remodeler, or developer evaluate the company's performance. Even though a remodeler would use the same ratio analysis, the target ratios will be different for a remodeling operation. For example, because of the risk factor involved in the unknown aspects of many remodeling jobs, the gross profit ratio should be significantly higher than in new construction.

$$\textbf{Gross Profit Ratio} = \frac{\textbf{Gross Profit}}{\textbf{Sales}}$$

In this ratio, gross profit equals sales less cost of sales. A good target gross profit ratio for new construction is generally between 25 and 30 percent. Remodelers should aim for a ratio between 35 and 45 percent depending on the nature of the remodeling operations and the unknown factors typically attributed to that particular segment of remodeling.

Marketing and financing expenses for remodeling are considerably less than for new construction. Generally, no commissions are involved in remodeling, and the owner or client secures the financing for the project. Remodelers who do pay sales commissions would allocate them to sales and marketing expenses.

Supervision and administrative costs are generally higher for remodeling companies than for new construction because the nature of remodeling requires closer supervision of the work to ensure client satisfaction. Indirect construction costs for a remodeling operation are generally treated as period expenses because remodeling jobs require no inventories. Therefore, remodelers do not need to allocate indirect costs to jobs. Because indirect construction costs are fixed in nature—meaning they do not fluctuate with changes in volume—they have to be controlled not only in relation to a budget or estimate established at the beginning of the year but also in relation to the actual volume of remodeled work.

Remodelers tend to use less subcontract labor and more payroll labor than do builders. The use of company employees to do the work can provide better control over the quality of the work and the honesty of the workforce. The use of company employees also requires more supervision to ensure adequate productivity.

In remodeling, the target for net profit before taxes should be from 10 to 15 percent, just as it is in new construction. Good management practices and proper accountability are common to both builders and remodelers. However, the relationship between the different elements contributing to profitability varies from new construction to remodeling. Therefore, accountability for remodeling activities must be separate from other activities to be able to evaluate the performance of the remodeling operation.

Chart of Accounts

The chart of accounts for a remodeling operation should be the same as the chart in Appendix A. The balance sheet accounts, assets, liability, and owners' equity apply to a remodeling operation. The income statement accounts, revenues, cost of sales, and expenses have been expanded to accommodate separate accounts in which to accumulate the accounting data from the remodeling activities. Appendices A and B list the recommended accounts and account numbers to accumulate revenues, cost of sales, and expenses of remodeling.

A company that is involved in more than one type of construction activity, for example new construction and remodeling, should treat the remodeling operation as a separate department or project. Refer to Chapter 11 for guidelines on how to account for the remodeling operation as a separate project.

Credit Approval

Unlike new construction, remodeling is, in most cases, financed by the owner without a financial institution or lender supervising the release of funds. Therefore, some type of credit-approval procedure must be in place to ensure full payment upon completion of the job.

There are several avenues to check the credit of a potential client depending on the size and dollar value of the job. Obtain a membership in a credit-rating company; it allows for a quick check on the credit worthiness of the potential client. Also make sure to follow up on credit references that the client provides.

On large jobs not financed by a lender, set up a joint account that (a) contains funds for the total amount of the contract and (b) requires signatures of both

owner and remodeler to release funds. The use of reputable escrow agents is another option available for large jobs. In addition, contracts must be very specific regarding payment terms and conditions for securing final payment. Many remodelers' contracts specify use of arbitrators in case of dispute.

Change orders should be monitored closely, as well as the suggestion that "since you are here, why don't you also take care of this little item." Collect payment for such services in advance of performing the work to ensure the client can pay. Make sure the client is at all times aware of the impact of changes on the total dollar amount for the job, and take precautions to avoid financial surprises upon completion of the job.

Job Costing

The control of construction costs for remodelers is essential to the profitability of the remodeling operation. The same principles discussed in Chapter 9 for home builders also apply to remodelers. An alternate way of accounting for cost of remodeling is to accumulate remodeling costs in Account 1430, direct construction cost instead of recording it as cost of sales in the 3800 series of accounts. The job cost subsidiary will accumulate the costs on a job-by-job basis using job cost accounts that provide points of control during the construction process. To record the actual costs, use the same job cost accounts used to estimate the jobs. This will facilitate variance analysis. Assign each job a number to identify it on the subsidiary record. All invoices should show the job number and the cost code as provided to the supplier at the time the order was placed.

The job cost subsidiary provides the foundation of the control system. Proper coding of invoices ensures that data collected by the job cost subsidiary is reliable. Refer to Chapter 9 for a detailed discussion of job costing concepts.

Completed Contracts

A small remodeling company maintaining accounting records on a cash basis records revenues from remodeling operations at the time cash is collected and records the costs and expenses at the time it pays for such costs and expenses. Because inventories are not being created in remodeling, this method of recognizing income, costs, and expenses is acceptable and it simplifies the accounting function. However, for control purposes the cash method delays the processing of key financial information.

An alternative method to obtain more timely financial information is the accrual method of accounting. In addition, when also using the completed contract method, there is better matching of revenues with costs and expenses. When using the completed contract method of revenue recognition, the recognition of income and costs is postponed until the job is done. During the remodeling process, the cost is accumulated in Account 1430 and transfers to cost of sales at the time the work is completed. Payments collected during the remodeling process are accumulated in Account 2010, contract deposits, and transfer to the revenue account when the work is completed. This method provides a more accurate measure of profit because it matches revenues and costs for jobs completed.

CHAPTER 14

Financial Planning Structure

The financial plan or budget is a numerical representation of the planned course of action set by the builders, remodelers, and developers to provide direction and improve the coordination, and control functions of their businesses. Budgets need to be based on thorough research and analysis of data that takes into account not only internal resources but also general economic trends and opportunities.

Responsibility for the company's budget process rests with the builder, remodeler, and developer and the top management team. However, to ensure that the budget is accepted and carried out, employees should help prepare the part of the budget for which they are responsible and will be held accountable.

The advantages of financial planning are that it:

- formally establishes a company's objectives and policies
- enables the company to use available resources more efficiently and effectively
- helps to coordinate and control staff responsibilities within the firm
- directs capital toward the most profitable channels

- helps to control specific operations and expenditures
- serves as a communication device within the organization
- establishes a standard against which a builder, remodeler, or developer can evaluate the company's performance

For the budgeting process to succeed, you should meet the following requirements:

- Prepare the budget or financial plan prior to the period it covers. For a one-year plan, start at least two months prior to the beginning of the period. For example, if your company operates on a calendar year, begin planning in early November.
- Define lines of authority within the company as well as each employee's budgeting responsibilities.
- Make sure the accounting system provides, in addition to the standard set of financial statements (balance sheet and income statement), more detailed financial information to assist in the planning process, such as product mix, gross profit reports by units, variance reports, cash flows, etc.
- Use the same structure to set the budgets that is being used to accumulate the historical data to ensure comparability and facilitate analysis.
- Review the budget to assure compliance with the overall business objectives.
- Create flexibility with the budget process to be able to adjust quickly to unexpected conditions in the market place. Review the budget periodically to adapt it to new developments, such as increased prices, changed financial and economic conditions, or other changes in the assumptions under which the original plan was developed. When changing the budget, make sure to retain the original budget for reference.

Elements of a Budget

Figure 14–1 illustrates the flow of the budgeting process and the relationship between the different components of the profit plan. Following there is a series of schedules that will take you step by step through the budgeting process. Each schedule represents a component that will be incorporated into the overall profit plan.

Sales Plan

Schedule I, the sales plan, is the first step in the budgeting process (Figure 14–2). The sales manager (who also may be the builder, remodeler, or developer) is generally the best qualified to determine sales volume and sales mix. He or she should evaluate the market, establish the market share, and recommend to the builder, remodeler, or developer the sales volume and mix for the coming year. If your firm has a production manager, close communication is essential because production capacity sets constraints on the sales plan. For example, a company cannot sell more units, remodeling jobs, or lots than it is able to produce. The sales plan needs to be converted into a closing plan based on the length of the construction process and the estimated time when sold units will close.

Production Plan

The production plan consists of a group of budgets, each of which represents one of the basic construction cost categories:

- land and land development cost (Schedule II, Figure 14–3)
- direct construction cost
- indirect construction cost (Schedule III, Figure 14–4)

Schedule IV (Figure 14–5) summarizes the three construction cost categories.

Construction cost estimates are essential to a building company's general financial plan. They provide the yardstick to be used in evaluating actual performance. Because direct construction cost consumes about 50 to 68 percent of a company's total sales dollars, it is the largest single item affecting the company's profit goals. The percentage for remodelers is also around 50 percent. Land acquisition absorbs around 25 percent of a developer's total

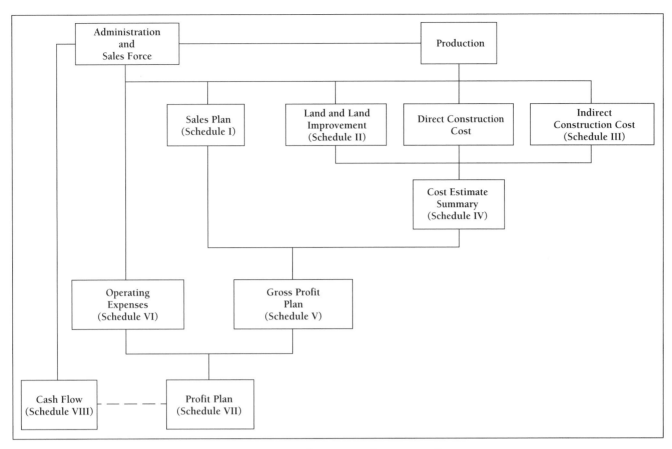

Figure 14–1. Planning information flow.

sales dollars and land development cost approximately 35 percent for a total of around 60 percent.

The purpose of estimating is not limited to pricing the house, lot, or remodeling job, but also to provide the yardstick against which to measure actual performance. The only way to ensure that an actual cost is in line with an estimate is to compare the two as work progresses. Therefore, use the same cost codes in estimating that are use in accumulating the actual cost. Each cost code thus, becomes a control point. Refer to Chapter 9 for further discussion on the job cost subsidiary and control system.

Date Prepared:

	January		February		March		Quarter Total			Year Total	
	Units	Amount	Units	Amount	Units	Amount	Units	Amount		Units	Amount
3050 Sales, Developed lots											
Average Sales Price											
3100 Sales, Single Family											
Average Sales Price											
Total Sales Revenue											
Record Schedule V											

Figure 14–2. Schedule I, sales plan—closings.

Date Prepared:

	Parcel A	Parcel B		Total
1320 Land for Development				
1410 Development Cost				
Financing and interest				
Realty Taxes				
Land Planning				
Engineering				
Rough Grading				
Streets				
Curb and Gutters				
Sidewalks				
Storm Sewers – Drainage				
Sanitary Sewers				
Water				
Electricity and Gas				
Amenities				
Other				
TOTAL				
A. Total Cost of Land Developed				
B. Number of lots				
C. Cost of Finished Lots				

Figure 14–3. Schedule II, land and land improvement plan.

Land and Land Development Costs

To arrive at an average cost per lot, builders and developers should accumulate the projected land and land development costs by parcel and then divide the total cost by the number of lots in each parcel (Figure 14–3, Schedule II). The computation of unit cost illustrated in Schedule II assumes that all lots in the parcel share land and land development costs in the same proportion. This method is the simplest one; other methods are discussed in detail in Chapter 15. Chapter 12 describes the special considerations relating to the land development process.

Direct Construction Costs

Builders, remodelers, and developers should budget direct construction costs in detail for each unit, job, or lot. Because during the planning process, the actual units that will be produced during the year might not be known, use the historical direct cost percentage or the percentage that is been set as a target for the year to estimate this cost category in the budgets. During the year as units are identified to go into production, prepare detail estimates for each unit.

Indirect Construction Costs

Indirect construction costs are budgeted for the year for the entire operation. These costs can be allocated to production units by using a predetermined rate based on the relationship of total estimated indirect construction costs to total estimated direct construction costs (Figure 14–4, Schedule III). Using the rate, the indirect costs can then be allocated to the units closed during each month. Re-

Date Prepared:

Cost Element	January	February	March	Quarter Totals		Year Total
4000 Salaries and Wages						
4100 Payroll Taxes and Benefits						
4200 Field Office Expenses						
4300 Field Warehouse and Storage						
4400 Construction Vehicles						
4500 Construction equipment						
4600 Unsold Units & under construction						
4700 Warranty and Customer Service						
4800 Depreciation Expense, Field						
4900 Other						
TOTAL						

Allocation of INDIRECT CONSTRUCTION COST:
    A. Total Direct Construction Cost (Per estimated percentage based on sales volume)
    B. Total Indirect Construction cost
    C. % of Indirect to Direct (B/A)
Note: This percentage is to be applied against the Direct Construction Cost per month.
    Record on Cost Estimate Summary, SCHEDULE IV)

Figure 14–4. Schedule III, indirect construction cost estimate.

fer to Chapter 7 for more information on how to account for indirect construction cost.

Cost Estimate Summary

The cost estimate summary accumulates the three construction cost categories to show the total cost for units closed each month. (Figure 14–5, Schedule IV).

Gross Profit Plan

The gross profit plan (Figure 14–6, Schedule V) interrelate the sales plan and the production plans. The gross profit plan establishes the contribution each product line will produce when sold by comparing the proposed sales price to the estimated cost.

Operating Expenses Plan

The operating expenses plan estimates the company's non-construction expenses commonly known as operating expenses (Figure 14–7, Schedule VI). The operating expenses include marketing, financing, and administrative expenses. They are budgeted by accounting period rather than allocated to units closed.

Profit Plan

The profit plan portrays the operations of a company during a projected period (Figure 14–8, Schedule VII). In other words, the profit plan presents in numbers a company's goals and objectives for the next calendar or fiscal period. The combined efforts of the owner, the sales manager, and the production manager provide the figures presented in the profit plan. The data appear in summarized form properly backed up by Schedules I to VI.

Date Prepared:

Cost Element	January	February	March	Quarter Totals		Year Total
1420 Finished lots (Schedule II)						
1430 Direct Construction Cost						
(Historical or target %)						
1440 Indirect Construction Cost						
(% of Direct Cost)						
TOTAL COST (Record SCHEDULE V)						

Figure 14–5. Schedule IV, cost estimate summary.

Date Prepared:

	January	February	March	Quarter Totals		Year Total
LOTS:						
3050 Sales, developed lots						
3550 Cost of Sales , developed lots						
GROSS PROFIT						
HOUSES:						
3100 Sales, Single family						
3600 Cost of Sales, single family						
Finished Lot Cost						
Direct Construction Cost						
Indirect Construction Cost						
GROSS PROFIT						
TOTAL GROSS PROFIT (Record SCHEDULE VII)						

NOTE: Sales figures are transferred from SCHEDULE I, Cost of Sales figures from SCHEDULE IV.

Figure 14–6. Schedule V, gross profit plan by product line.

Date prepared:

Cost Element	January	February	March	Quarter Totals		Year Total
5000 FINANCING EXPENSES						
5020 Interest on notes and mortgages						
5040 Interest on construction loans						
5090 Other financing expense						
5120 Fees						
5130 Appraisal and related fees						
5140 Inspection fees						
5210 Closing costs						
5220 Title and recording						
5230 Fees, commitments						
TOTAL FINANCING EXPENSES Record SCHEDULE VII						
6000 SALES AND MARKETING						
6000 Salaries – Sales personnel						
6100 Payroll taxes and benefits						
6200 Sales office expense						
6300 Advertising and sales promotion						
6400 Sales vehicles, travel, entertainment						
6600 Model Home expense						
6700 Sales and marketing fees						
6800 Depreciation, Sales						
6900 Other sales and marketing expenses						
TOTAL SALES AND MARKETING Record SCHEDULE VII						
8000 GENERAL & ADMINISTRATIVE						
8000 Salaries – G&A						
8100 Payroll taxes and benefits						
8200 Office expenses						
8300 Computer expenses						
8400 Vehicles, travel and entertainment						
8500 Taxes						
8600 Insurance						
8700 Professional services						
8800 Depreciation, G&A						
8900 Other General and administrative						
TOTAL G & A EXPENSES Record SCHEDULE VII						
TOTAL OPERATING EXPENSES						

Figure 14–7. Schedule VI, operating expenses plan.

Date Prepared:

	January	February	March	Quarter Totals		Year Total
3000 Sales (SCHEDULE I)						
3500 Cost of Sales (SCHEDULE IV						
Gross Profit (SCHEDULE V)						
Operating Expenses:						
5000 Financing (SCHEDULE VI)						
6000 Sales & Marketing (SCHEDULE VI)						
8000 G & A (SCHEDULE VI)						
Total Operating						
Net Operating Profit (Loss)						
9100 Other Income						
9200 Other Expense						
Net Income (loss) before Income Tax						

NOTE: The income tax provision will be dependent upon the organization structure of the company. (Sole proprietorship, partnership, corporation, etc.)

Figure 14–8. Schedule VII, profit plan.

Schedule VII refers to the schedules from which the data were obtained. In some small-volume firms the sales manager and the production manager are the same person. In others, the builder, remodeler or developer might also be the sales manager and/or the production manager.

Cash Flow Report

The cash flow report (Figure 14–9, Schedule VIII) is a powerful tool a builder, remodeler, or developer has for cash planning and control. The cash flow report identifies all possible sources and uses of cash and predicts within which period the company will receive or need the cash.

The key point in preparing a cash flow projection is the transfer of cash rather than the financial transaction. For example, signing an option contract or closing a sales contract does not necessarily determine when cash is to be received. In some areas of the country, money is not transferred at the closing;

it occurs several days later. In cash planning this lag can be significant. Similarly, the date materials are purchased is not important, instead the crucial date is when the invoice must be paid.

Builders, remodelers, and developers operating on relatively small cash balances may want to prepare weekly cash flow reports. Businesses with large cash reserves might require cash flow reports only on a monthly basis. (See Chapter 8 for additional information on cash flow analysis.)

Reports

The greatest benefit of financial planning is to use the budgets created through the planning process as a yardstick to measure actual performance.

Financial reports should compare actual results with the plan or budget for the same period.

Financial reports will be more effective if they:

Date Prepared:

	January	February	March	Quarter Totals		Year Total
BEGINNING CASH BALANCE						
RECEIPTS						
Cash Sales						
Collection on receivables						
Deposits by customers						
Construction loans						
Total Receipts						
Total Available Cash						
DISBURSEMENTS						
Payment of Accounts Payable						
Payroll – net						
Payroll taxes						
Construction loans						
Income Taxes						
Real Estate taxes						
Land purchases						
Interest						
TOTAL DISBURSEMENTS						
Cash excess (or shortage)						
CASH REQUIREMENTS						
Borrowed Funds needed						
Repayment of borrowed funds						
ENDING CASH BALANCE						

Figure 14–9. Schedule VIII, cash flow.

- Allow owners or managers to measure the performance of each functional area of the company and at the same time relate it to the manager responsible for each function.
- Are timely. In other words, builders, remodelers, and developers should receive reports to allow for prompt action to correct unfavorable developments indicated by the reports.
- Compare actual results with the plan or budget for each line item on the report.
- Highlight deviations from the plan.
- Are dependable, accurate, and easy to use.

Wherever possible the format of the reports should be standardized to facilitate comparisons and analysis.
- Are customized to match the management level. In large companies, top managers should receive summary reports and lower-level managers, who are responsible for achieving specific goals, get detailed reports that back up the summarized reports. Top managers will always have access to detail information when requested.
- Provide benefits that outweigh the cost of preparing the report.

Technical Aspects of Accounting

This chapter discusses several aspects of an accounting system for builders, remodelers, and developers that are often misunderstood. It provides some insight into what generally accepted accounting procedures (GAAP) and what the Internal Revenue Service (IRS) codes specify. Whenever possible the information includes the current policies of the National Association of Home Builders (NAHB) on these issues. Because tax laws are subject to rapid and frequent change, you should consult a qualified accounting or tax expert if you have any doubts about the current requirements.

Land Acquisition and Development

Pre-acquisition Costs

Builders and developers often incur costs related to a property prior to taking title to it. These pre-acquisition costs would include options to purchase, engineering and architectural fees, and expenses for feasibility studies.

The pre-acquisition costs involved with purchasing a tract or parcel of land must be capitalized if they are to meet the four basic criteria of Financial Accounting Standards Board (FASB) Statement No. 67.

- Costs can be directly identified with a specific project.
- Costs would be capitalized if the property were already acquired.
- Acquisition of the property is probable.
- The total capitalized costs do not exceed the net realizable value of the property.

Developers should accumulate these costs initially in Account 1320, land held for development. They should debit them to Account 1410, land and land development, at the time land development begins and credit them to Account 1320. They should expense any costs that do not meet these criteria. If a potential acquisition does not work out, they should expense all previously capitalized costs related to that acquisition attempt.

Acquisition Costs

Land acquisition costs include purchase price, legal fees, sales commission, appraisals, recording and other closing fees, zoning and planning costs, and interest if a mortgage note is involved. All land acquisition costs should be capitalized to the cost basis of the land. If the parcel of land is held for "investment," future opportunities, land banking, or any other reason by which the land parcel will not go into development until some future time, the interest on the acquisition loan will be expensed until such time when the development process starts. It is only during the construction/development period that the interest and other carrying costs are capitalized for book and tax purposes.

Account 1320 is the initial accumulation account. When development starts, these costs should be transferred by debiting Account 1410 and crediting Account 1320.

If you will not be developing a tract of land you acquired for development, you must take two steps.

First, you must compare the total cost of the land with the estimated realizable net value of the land. Second, you must expense the costs in excess of value in that accounting period.

Land Development Costs

Land development costs include planning, design and engineering studies, earthwork (grading, excavation, etc.), utility line installation, streets, curbs, gutters, and sidewalks. See Appendix G, Land Development Cost Subsidiary Ledger. The costs that you can identify with the land must be capitalized.

Your initial accumulation point for such costs should be Account 1410. Upon completion of each tract, you would debit a pro rata share of costs for each lot to Account 1420, developed lots, and credit them to Account 1410. Determining the pro rata share for individual lots or phases of projects requires a method of allocation. Paragraph 11 of FASB No. 67 states that whenever possible you should make the direct allocation by identifying the individual component of construction. Direct allocation is possible when the builder develops individual lots on scattered sites. Most of these are small-scale operations. When such individual identification is not practical—for example, in subdivision tract acquisition and development—then you should allocate land costs to each component (lot or tract phase) of the project based on one of the following methods:

- The fair market value of the land after development but before construction. (Fair market value is determined at the time of allocation.) Assigning a fair market value at this stage is difficult; therefore, if this timing is impractical, paragraph 11 will permit allocation of capitalized costs based on area methods.
- The square-footage allocation method (the most popular area method).

At each lot closing this pro rata calculation produces the amount to be transferred from Account 1420 to Account 3550, cost of sales, developed lots, or to the appropriate cost of sales account (3500–3700) depending on the type of lot that closed.

Type of property	Minimum investment (percentage of sales)
Single-family residential property	
• Primary residence of buyer	5%
• Secondary or recreational residence	10
Land	
• Held for residential development to commence within two years of sale	20
• Held for residential development to commence after two years	25
Multifamily residential property	
• Primary residence	
Cash flow sufficient to service debt	10
Start up situation or insufficient cash flow to service debt	15
• Secondary or recreational residence	
Cash flow sufficient to service debt	15
Start up situation or insufficient cash flow to service debt	25

Figure 15–1. Minimum initial investment chart.

Accounting for Amenities

Paragraph 8 of FASB No. 67 states that accounting for the costs of amenities such as swimming pools, golf courses, and tennis courts can be handled in one of two ways, depending on the intention of the builder or developer. If the amenity is to be turned over at a later date to the homeowner's association as a "common element," you should allocate the costs of construction to units as they are sold. If you plan to sell the amenity or retain title to it you should allocate to the individual units only the costs in excess of fair market value.

Frequently, costs must be estimated because the amenities are not always complete when units are ready for settlement. You must accrue these estimated costs as a liability and debit them to inventory. At closing, you transfer the inventory to cost of sales and include a pro rata share of the unfinished work.

Carrying Costs

Some confusion exists within the building industry about the methods of accounting for general carrying charges. Carrying charges include interest, other financing costs, and property taxes. In both cases most builders and developers capitalize these costs until the construction period is complete. After this point, you can either capitalize them or expense them in accordance with IRS Code Section 266.

Section 266 gives the developer/builder the option via the following criteria:

• For unimproved real property, an election (to capitalize or expense) is binding for the year of the election only.
• For property being developed the option still exists, but once the election is made it is binding until the completion of the development.

Direct Construction Costs

Direct construction costs include permits, labor, materials, subcontractors, construction period interest, and any other costs directly related to the construction of a particular job or unit. The NAHB Chart of Accounts accumulates these costs in Account 1430, direct construction costs. A subsidiary ledger that summarizes the costs of construction for each unit must support this account. (See Appendix E, which contains the NAHB-recommended Chart of Accounts for the direct construction cost subsidiary ledger.)

Upon completion of a unit, you should issue a credit to Account 1430 and a debit to Account 1510, finished units. On closing the unit you would credit the 1510 account and debit the appropriate costs of sales account.

Builders who develop their own lots should segregate the lot and structure costs. Careful accumulation of these costs allows you to monitor the variances from the budgeted estimates. The system allows you to measure the strengths and weaknesses of each land development and construction project.

Paragraph 7 of FASB No. 67 addresses the accounting requirements for direct and indirect construction costs:

- Project costs clearly associated with the acquisition, development, and construction of a real estate project shall be capitalized as a cost of that project. Indirect project costs that relate to several projects shall be capitalized and allocated to the projects to which the costs relate. Indirect costs that do not clearly relate to projects under development or construction, including general and administrative expenses, shall be charged to expense as incurred.

Indirect Construction Costs

Indirect construction costs are the necessary costs of construction that cannot be directly, easily, or economically attributed to a specific unit of construction. Examples of these indirect costs include salaries of construction superintendents, general laborers, cost for field offices, temporary utilities, construction vehicles, and on-site portable sanitation facilities.

You should accumulate all indirect costs in Account 1440, indirect construction costs, and support this

account with a subsidiary ledger that summarizes the indirect construction costs for a project or period, whichever is appropriate. Appendix F provides the NAHB-recommended outline of a subsidiary chart of accounts for indirect construction costs. For management reasons many builders prefer to accumulate indirect costs as operating expenses while the expenses are being incurred (NAHB Chart of Accounts 4000 series). No matter which accumulation method you use to conform to IRS and GAAP requirements, you eventually must allocate all indirect construction costs to a specific unit of production (for example, a house, a remodeling job, or a lot).

The principle behind spreading or allocating indirect costs to individual units of production is to determine, as accurately as possible, the gross profit on each unit sold. Often the most practical procedure is to estimate the indirect construction costs at the beginning of a project or phase and allocate the estimated amount to each unit.

At the end of the fiscal period or upon completion of the project, you can reconcile the actual indirect costs with the allocated estimate and handle the variance with an adjusting entry at the end of the accounting period.

Builders, remodelers, and developers must look at their operations to determine the allocation method to apply. The five major methods of allocating indirect construction costs to costs of sales are described in the following paragraphs.

Sales Value Method. Builders often use this method when they are selling several different models in the same subdivision. With this method, first determine the number of units in the entire subdivision and the estimated sales value of each model group compared with the total estimated sales value of the subdivision to determine the percentage of total sales for each model group. Second, multiply this percentage by the total indirect construction costs to determine the allocation of indirect costs to this model group. Third, to calculate the indirect costs for each unit within the group, divide the total indirect costs for the model group by the number of units in the group.

Example 15-1:
Sales Value Method

	Number of Units	Estimated Sales Value	Percent of Total
Model A	5	$500,000	22
Model B	10	$800,000	35
Model C	15	$975,000	43
Total		$2,275,000	100

	Total Indirect Costs		Percent of Total		Group Total/ Units		Indirect Costs/ Unit
Model A	$300,000	×	22	=	$66,000 / 5	=	$13,200
Model B	$300,000	×	35	=	$105,000 / 10	=	$10,500
Model C	$300,000	×	43	=	$141,000 / 15	=	$9,400

Number-of-Units-Built Method. Using this method you would divide the total indirect costs by the total number of units built to determine an average indirect cost per unit. This method works accurately only where the same or very similar models are built.

Total-Direct-Costs Method. To use this most popular method, divide the total estimated direct cost of the unit by the total direct costs for all the units built to determine the percentage of total for the individual unit. Multiply this percentage by the total indirect construction costs for all the units to calculate the indirect cost for the unit.

Area Method. This method is often used in subdivisions in which the area of each unit varies. First, divide the total estimated indirect construction costs by the total area (square footage) of all the units in the project to get the cost per square foot. Second, multiply the cost per square foot by the actual number of square feet in each unit. This calculation produces the indirect costs allocated for each unit.

Percent of Indirect to Direct Cost Method. This popular method establishes a percentage relationship between indirect costs and direct costs. You calculate the allocation as a percentage of dollars spent for direct costs in each unit.

Consistency

A builder who repeatedly builds the same model might find the number-of-units-built method best, whereas a builder of a diversified product line might find the percentage-of-direct construction-costs method best, and a multifamily builder would probably use the area method. Consistency is the most important requirement for meeting IRS "reasonable" allocation standards.

Example 15-2:
Number of Units Built

$$\frac{\text{Total indirect costs}}{\text{Units to be built}} = \frac{\$300,000}{30} = \$10,000 \text{ Allocation to each unit}$$

Example 15-3:
Total Direct Costs

$$\frac{\text{Total direct costs of unit 1}}{\text{Units to be built}} = \frac{\$50,000}{1,000,000} = 0.05 \text{ (5\%)}$$

Total indirect costs	$300,000
Unit % of total direct costs	× .05 (5%)
Allocation to unit 1	$15,000

When you make year-end adjustments to correct estimates of indirect costs, you should use the same method of allocation that you used during the year. You should also strive for consistency between projects.

Sales and Marketing Expenses

Under certain circumstances, some sales and marketing costs will need to be capitalized. To capitalize sales and marketing costs, the costs must meet two criteria as outlined in paragraph 17 of FASB No. 67:

- You must reasonably expect to recover the costs.
- The costs must relate to a tangible asset that is used throughout the sales period (for example, a model home).

Examples of capitalized sales and marketing costs are model homes and their furnishings, sales facilities, and semipermanent signs. Examples of marketing and sales costs that you should expense as you incur them include media advertising, salesperson overhead (including salaries), and gala event promotions.

Revenue Recognition

FASB Statement No. 66, Real Estate Sales Other Than Retail Land Sales, provides insight into the application of GAAP in accounting for revenues resulting from sales of homes, buildings, parcels of land, sales of lots to builders, sales of options to acquire real estate, sales of time-sharing interests in real estate, and sales of corporate stock or partnership interests in which the transaction is actually a real estate transfer.

GAAP requires the realization of revenue in the period in which earnings are substantially complete and the exchange has taken place. These revenues are usually recognized at the amount established by the parties to the exchange, except when collection of receivables is not reasonably assured. An explanation of the accepted methods of accounting for these revenues follows.

Full Accrual Method

Under the full accrual method, you would recognize income at the time of sale. It is often mistak-

---

Example 15-4:
Area Method

$$\frac{\text{Total estimated indirect costs}}{\text{Area of all units (sq. ft.)}} = \frac{\$300,000}{45,000} = \$6.67/\text{sq. ft.}$$

Total area of unit 1	2,000 sq. ft.
Indirect cost per foot	× $6.67
Allocated to unit 1	$13,340

Example 15-5:
Percentage Method

$$\frac{Total\ estimated\ indirect\ costs}{Total\ estimated\ direct\ costs} = \frac{\$90,000}{\$1,000,000} = 0.09\ (9\%)$$

Total direct costs of unit 1	$50,000
Times indirect cost %	× .03 (3%)
Indirect cost allocation to unit 1	$4,500

enly called the completed contract method. However, that method requires you to recognize income when a contract is considered complete or substantially complete. The full accrual method is a modified completed contract approach.

Because the full accrual method requires you to recognize all revenue at closing, you accrue all related costs in the cost of sales for the same period. If a unit is partially complete at year end, the related costs remain in inventory and no revenue is recognized. If a completed unit is unsold at the end of a period, the costs remain in Account 1510 and you would not recognize any revenue.

You have consummated a sale (a) when you and the buyer have met all conditions preceding closing (including arrangement of permanent financing by the buyer) and (b) when you and the buyer have exchanged all considerations related to the sale and title has passed.

The full accrual method has one exception that allows you to recognize income prior to the closing of a sale, but you must meet two criteria:

• You must be able to determine the amount of profit and be reasonably sure you will collect it.
• The work must be substantially completed.

You must meet three basic criteria for using the full accrual method for the normal closing of a residential unit:

• You must close a sale.
• The buyer's investment must be sufficient to demonstrate a commitment to pay for the property.

• The seller must have transferred the usual risks and rewards of ownership to the buyer. The seller must not have a substantial continuing involvement with the property.

For a buyer's investment to adequately demonstrate a commitment to pay for the property, the buyer must make a minimum initial investment or down payment of either (a) a set percentage of the sales value based on the type of transaction (Figure 15–1) or (b) the lesser of the difference between the sales value and 115 percent of the buyer's permanent mortgage loan or 15 percent of the sales value of the property.

For example, a new home goes to closing with a sales price of $150,000 and a permanent mortgage loan of $125,000 secured by the buyer through an independent lending institution. The home will be the primary residence of the buyer. Under the full accrual method, FASB 66 provides that the minimum down payment from the buyer should be the greater of 1 or 2 below:

1. The percentage of the sales value, as indicated in Figure 15–1, is $7,500 (5% of $150,000)
2. a. The difference between the sales value and 115 percent of the permanent mortgage loan is $6,250 (115% of $125,000 = $143,750, and $150,000 − $143,750 = $6,250)
   b. The sales value multiplied by 25 percent is $37,500 ($150,000 × 25% = $37,500).

The lesser amount between 2a ($6,250) and 2b ($37,500) is $6,250. The greater amount between 2a ($6,250) and 1 ($7,500) is $7,500. Therefore, the minimum down payment must be $7,500.

The usual risks and rewards of ownership are considered transferred when the seller no longer has a substantial continuing interest in the property and/or all of the obligations of the contract have been met. Full performance removes the seller's receivable if one exists from possible future subordination to any other lien holder.

Percentage of Completion Method

In the percentage of completion method, you should recognize income throughout the life of a project contract based on a periodic (usually annual) measurement of progress toward completion. Obviously, this method has potential for builders of commercial and industrial projects that take longer to complete.

From the homebuilding perspective, application of the percentage of completion has limitations. FASB 66 permits the use of this method with high-rise condominium and timesharing units. Revenue recognition for low-rise condominiums differs from that for high-rise condominiums because you can complete a low-rise, cluster condominium and obtain a certificate of occupancy for it before substantially completing the rest of the subdivision. For these low-rise projects, you should use the full accrual method and recognize the profit at closing time.

Paragraph 73 of FASB 66 states that in the percentage of completion method:

The earnings process is not complete if a seller is obliged to complete improvements of lots sold or to construct amenities and other facilities applicable to lots sold, if those obligations are significant in relation to total costs, and if they remain unperformed at the time the sale is recognized. Therefore, the amount of revenue recognized at the time of sale is measured by the relationship of costs already incurred to total estimated costs to be incurred, including costs of the marketing effort.

Paragraph 75 defines estimated costs as being based upon costs generally expected in the local construction market. These estimates are to be reviewed at least annually. Changes in these estimates do not lead to adjustment of revenue previously recorded unless the adjusted total cost exceeds applicable revenue.

Cost Recovery Method

When you cannot reasonably assess the ability to collect the sales price from the buyer or when the sales price is contingent, for example, on availability of a special kind of material or on foundation requirements subject to unusual soil conditions, the cost recovery method may be practical. In this method the amounts collected are first applied against costs incurred. After recovery of an amount equal to the total costs incurred, the receipts are treated as income.

Deposit Method

The deposit method can be used when you are highly uncertain about whether you can collect the sales price. In this method, sellers retain the property on their books as an asset. Cash receipts are shown as a liability. Cash received as nonrefundable interest can be used to offset existing carrying charges on the property. The financial statements must disclose the transaction for the contract.

If a contract under the deposit method is canceled without a refund, the deposits forfeited are treated as income. When deposits received are eventually recognized as income, the interest portion is treated as interest income.

Other Sources of Information

This chapter is intended to clarify some of the more confusing issues of accounting for home builders, remodelers, and developers. If you need additional information, contact your accountant or call the

NAHB Builder Business Services Department. It maintains a listing of industry financial consultants who can assist builders with many of their accounting and financial management needs. Another source of information is the Web, particularly www.irs.gov, the Website for the IRS, and www.fasb.org, the Website for the Financial Accounting Standards Board.

Part A. Outline of NAHB Chart of Accounts

1000–1990	**Assets**
1000–1090	**Cash**
1010	Petty cash
1020	Cash on deposit, general
1030	Cash on deposit, payroll
1040	Cash on deposit, savings and money market
1050	Cash on deposit, held in escrow
1100–1190	**Short-term Investments**
1110	Certificates of Deposit
1120	Marketable securities
1130	Government securities
1190	Other short-term investments
1200–1290	**Receivables**
1210	Accounts receivable, trade
1220	Accounts receivable, other
1230	Notes receivable
1250	Mortgage notes receivable, current year
1260	Due on construction and development loans

1270   Accrued interest receivable
1280   Allowance for doubtful accounts
1290   Retentions (retainage) receivable

1300–1390   Inventories
1310   Construction materials inventory
1320   Land held for development
1330   Property held for Remodeling

1400–1490   Construction Work in Progress
1410   Land and land development
1412   Accumulated allocations, land and land development costs
1420   Developed lots
1430   Direct construction cost
1440   Indirect construction cost
1470   Cost in excess of billings

1500–1590   Finished Units and Other Inventory
1510   Finished units
1520   Model homes
1530   Trade-ins and repossessions

1600–1690   Other Current Assets
1610   Refundable deposits
1620   Prepaid expenses
1630   Employee advances
1650   Due from affiliated companies or subsidiaries
1660   Due from officers, stockholders, owners or partners
1670   Deposits on plans
1690   Other current assets

1700–1790   Investments and Other Assets
1710   Investments, long-term
1720   Cash surrender value of officers' life insurance
1730   Investments in affiliated entities
1750   Mortgage notes receivable, long-term
1760   Due from affiliated companies or subsidiaries, long-term
1770   Due from officers, owners, stockholders, long-term
1780   Organization cost

1800–1890   Property, Plant, and Equipment
1810   Land
1820   Buildings
1825   Rental property
1827   Recreation amenities
1830   Office furniture and equipment
1840   Vehicles
1850   Construction equipment

1870   Model home furnishings
1880   Leasehold improvements
1890   Computer equipment and software

1900–1990   Accumulated Depreciation
1920   Accumulated depreciation, buildings
1925   Accumulated depreciation, rental properties
1927   Accumulated depreciation, recreation amenities
1930   Accumulated depreciation, office furniture and equipment
1940   Accumulated depreciation, vehicles
1950   Accumulated depreciation, construction equipment
1970   Accumulated depreciation, model home furnishings
1980   Accumulated depreciation, leasehold improvements
1990   Accumulated depreciation, computer equipment and software

2000–2990   Liabilities and Owners' Equity
2000–2090   Deposits by Customers
2010   Contract deposits
2030   Tenant security deposit
2040   Advance rent collected

2100–2190   Accounts Payable
2110   Accounts payable, trade
2120   Retentions payable
2190   Accounts payable, other

2200–2290   Notes Payable
2200   Line of credit payable
2220   Acquisitions and development loans payable (old 252 in prior accounts)
2230   Construction loans payable
2240   Current portion of long-term debt
2290   Notes payable, other

2300–2490   Other Current Liabilities
2310   Social Security and Medicare
2320   Federal payroll tax withheld and accrued
2330   State payroll tax withheld and accrued
2340   Other payroll withholdings
2345   Union withholding and benefits payable
2350   Sales and use taxes payable
2360   Real estate taxes payable
2370   Income taxes payable
2390   Accrued interest payable
2400   Accrued salaries and wages payable
2410   Accrued commissions payable
2411   Accrued pension and profit-sharing expenses

2420 Workers' Compensation insurance payable
2425 Other accrued expenses
2430 Deferred income
2440 Due to affiliated companies or subsidiaries
2450 Due to officers, stockholders, owners, and partners
2480 Billings in excess of costs
2490 Other current liabilities

2500–2890   Long-term Liabilities
2510 Long-term notes payable
2530 Mortgage notes payable
2600 Deferred income tax payable
2610 Due to affiliated companies or subsidiaries, long-term
2620 Due to officers, stockholders, owners, long-term, and partners
2700 Other long-term liabilities

2900–2990   Owners' Equity
2900 Common stock
2910 Additional paid in capital
2920 Retained earnings
2930 Treasury stock
2940 Unrealized holding gain
2950 Partnership or proprietorship account
2960 Distributions, dividends, and draws

3000–3990   Sales, Revenues, and Cost of Sales

3000–3490   Sales and Revenues
3000 Sales, land held for development
3050 Sales, developed lots
3100 Sales, single-family speculative
3110 Sales, single-family production
3120 Sales, single-family custom designed
3125 Sales, single-family custom designed, no land
3130 Sales, residential remodeling
3133 Sales, commercial and industrial remodeling
3135 Sales, insurance restoration
3137 Sales, repairs
3140 Sales, multifamily
3150 Sales, commercial and industrial
3160 Sales, trade-ins, and repossessions
3190 Sales, other
3200 Rental property income
3210 Common area reimbursements
3220 Other reimbursements
3230 Parking fee income
3240 Amenities and facilities income

3360 Construction management fee income
3370 Design fees collected
3400 Miscellaneous income
3410 Interest income
3420 Dividend income
3450 Earned discounts
3490 Sales concessions and discounts

3500–3790   Cost of Sales
3500 Cost of sales, land held for development
3550 Cost of sales, developed lots
3600 Cost of sales, single-family speculative
3610 Cost of sales, single-family production
3620 Cost of sales, single-family custom designed
3625 Cost of sales, single-family custom designed, no land
3630 Cost of sales, remodeling
3633 Cost of sales, commercial and industrial remodeling
3635 Cost of sales, insurance restoration
3637 Cost of sales, repairs
3640 Cost of sales, multifamily
3650 Cost of sales, commercial and industrial
3660 Cost of sales, trade-ins
3690 Cost of sales, other
3700 Direct construction cost for prior periods

3800–3899   Costs of Construction— Remodeling
3810 Direct labor
3820 Labor burden
3830 Building material
3840 Subcontractors
3850 Rental equipment
3860 Other direct construction costs
3870 Professional design fees

4000–4990   Indirect Construction Cost

4000–4090   Salaries and Wages
4010 Superintendents
4020 Laborers
4030 Production manager
4040 Architects, drafters, estimators, and purchasers
4050 Other indirect construction wages

4100–4190   Payroll Taxes and Benefits
4110 Payroll taxes
4120 Workers' Compensation insurance
4130 Health and accident insurance
4140 Retirement, pension, and profit sharing
4150 Union benefits

4190   Other benefits

4200–4290   Field Office Expenses

4210   Rent, field office

4230   Repairs and maintenance, field office

4250   Utilities, field office

4260   Telephone, field office

4265   Mobile phones, pagers, and radios

4290   Other field office expenses

4300–4390   Field Warehouse and Storage Expenses

4310   Rent, field warehouse and storage

4330   Repairs and maintenance, field warehouse and storage

4350   Utilities, field warehouse and storage

4360   Telephone, field warehouse and storage

4400–4490   Construction Vehicles, Travel, and Entertainment

4410   Lease payments, construction vehicles

4420   Mileage reimbursement

4430   Repairs and maintenance, construction vehicles

4440   Operating expenses, construction vehicles

4450   Taxes, licenses, and insurance, construction vehicles

4460   Travel, construction department

4470   Customer business entertainment, construction

4480   Training and education, construction

4490   Recruiting fees and expenses, construction

4500–4590   Construction Equipment

4510   Rent, construction equipment

4530   Repairs and maintenance, construction equipment

4540   Operating expenses, construction equipment

4550   Taxes and insurance, construction equipment

4560   Small tools and supplies

4600–4690   Expenses for Maintaining Unsold Units and Units Under Construction

4610   Temporary utilities

4620   Trash maintenance

4640   Lawn care

4650   Utilities, completed units

4660   Repairs and maintenance, completed units

4700–4790   Warranty and Customer Service

4710   Salaries and wages, warranty

4720   Material, warranty

4730   Subcontractor, warranty

4790   Other, warranty expenses

4800–4890   Depreciation Expenses

4820   Depreciation, construction office

4830   Depreciation, warehouse

4840   Depreciation, construction vehicles

4850   Depreciation, construction equipment

4900–4990   Other

4910   Insurance and bonding expenses

4920   Builders risk insurance

4990   Absorbed indirect costs

5000–5990   Financing Expenses

5000–5090   Interest

5010   Interest on line of credit

5020   Interest on notes payable

5030   Interest expense on developed lots

5040   Interest incurred on construction loans

5050   Interest on completed inventory

5090   Interest expense, Other

5100–5190   Construction Loan Points and Fees

5120   Points and fees

5130   Appraisal and related fees

5140   Inspection fees

5200–5290   Closing Costs

5210   Closing costs

5220   Title and recording

5230   Fees, commitment

6000–6990   Sales and Marketing Expenses

6000–6090   Sales Salaries and Commissions

6010   Sales manager's compensation

6030   Salaries, sales personnel

6040   Sales commissions, in-house

6050   Sales commissions, outside

6090   Other sales office salaries and wages

6100–6190   Payroll Taxes and Benefits, Sales and Marketing

6110   Payroll taxes, sales and marketing

6120   Workers' Compensation insurance, sales and marketing

6130   Health and accident insurance, sales and marketing

6140   Retirement, pension, and profit-sharing plans, sales and marketing

6190   Other benefits

6200–6290   Sales Office Expenses

6210   Rent, sales office

6230   Repairs and maintenance, sales office

6250   Utilities, sales office

6260 Telephone, sales office

6270 Supplies, sales office

6300–6390 Advertising and Sales Promotion

6310 Print advertising

6320 Radio advertising

6325 Television advertising

6330 Internet fees, web page design, and maintenance costs

6340 Brochures and catalogues

6350 Signs

6355 Billboards

6365 Promotions

6370 Agency commissions

6380 Multiple listing fees

6390 Public relations

6395 Referral fees

6400–6490 Sales Vehicles, Travel, and Entertainment

6410 Lease payments, sales vehicles

6420 Mileage reimbursement

6430 Repairs and maintenance, sales vehicles

6440 Operating expenses, sales vehicles

6450 Taxes, licenses, insurance, sales vehicles

6460 Travel, sales and marketing

6470 Customer business entertainment

6600–6690 Model Home Maintenance

6610 Rent or lease payments, model home furnishings

6620 Model home rent or lease payments

6625 Model home decorating fees

6630 Repairs and maintenance, model homes

6650 Utilities, model homes

6670 Lawn and landscaping care model homes

6680 Cleanup, model homes

6690 Interest on model homes

6700–6790 Sales and Marketing Fees

6710 Market research and consultation

6720 Interior design fee

6770 Recruiting fees and expenses, sales and marketing personnel

6780 Training and education expenses

6800–6890 Depreciation

6810 Depreciation, sales office

6830 Depreciation, sales vehicles

6870 Depreciation, model home furnishings, and decorations

6900–6990 Other Marketing Expenses

6930 Sales concessions

6940 Buydowns

6999 Other sales and marketing expenses

7000–7990 Operating and Management Expenses, Rental Operations

7000–7090 Property Management

7010 Property manager's compensation

7030 Salaries and wages, property management personnel

7040 Commissions, in-house

7050 Commissions, outside

7060 Salaries and wages to maintenance personnel

7070 Payroll taxes and benefits, rental operations

7072 Workers' Compensation insurance, rental

7073 Health and accident insurance, rental

7074 Retirement, pension, and profit-sharing plans, rental

7079 Other benefits, rental

7100–7190 Rental Expenses

7110 Advertising

7130 Credit reports

7190 Other rental expenses

7200–7290 Administrative Expenses, Rental Operations

7220 Management and service fees

7230 Office expenses

7240 Telephone

7250 Tenant bad debts

7260 Collection costs

7290 Other administrative expenses

7300–7390 Professional Services, Rental Operations

7310 Legal services

7320 Accounting services

7330 Market research

7390 Other professional services, rental operations

7400–7490 Operating Expenses, Rental Operations

7410 Utilities

7420 Engineering

7430 Janitorial

7440 Trash removal service

7450 Exterminating

7460 Snow removal

7470 Other contractual services

7480 Vehicles and equipment, rental operations

7490 Other rental operations expenses

7500–7590 Taxes and Insurance, Rental Operations

7510 Real estate property taxes

7520 Personal property taxes

7530 Franchise taxes

7540 License fees

7560 Workers' Compensation insurance

7570 Insurance, rental operations

7590 Other taxes and insurance, rental operations

7690 Maintenance and Repairs, Rental Operations

7610 Tenant redecorating

7630 Maintenance contracts and services

7640 Ground maintenance and repairs

7650 Vehicle maintenance and repairs, rental operations

7660 Equipment maintenance and repairs, rental operations

7670 Amenities maintenance and repairs

7700–7790 Financing Expense, Rental Operations

7710 Interest on mortgage payable

7720 Interest on long-term notes payable

7800–7890 Depreciation Expenses, Rental Operations

7810 Depreciation, building

7820 Depreciation, maintenance equipment

7830 Depreciation, vehicles

7840 Depreciation, furniture and fixtures

7850 Depreciation, amenities

7890 Other Depreciation

7900–7990 Other Management and Operating Expenses

8000–8990 General and Administrative Expense

8000–8090 Salaries and Wages

8010 Salaries, owners

8020 Salaries, officers

8030 Salaries, management

8050 Salaries and wages, office and clerical

8090 Other general and administrative salaries and wages

8100–8190 Payroll Taxes and Benefits

8110 Payroll taxes

8120 Workers' Compensation insurance

8130 Health and accident insurance

8140 Retirement, pension, and profit-sharing plans

8190 Other employee benefits

8200–8290 Office Expenses

8210 Rent

8220 Office equipment rental

8230 Repairs and maintenance, administrative office space

8240 Repairs and maintenance, administrative office equipment

8250 Utilities, administrative office

8260 Telephone, administrative office

8270 Office supplies, administrative office

8280 Postage and deliveries

8290 Miscellaneous expenses, administrative office

8300–8390 Computer Expenses

8310 Computer supplies

8320 Leases, computer hardware

8330 Leases, computer software

8350 Repairs and maintenance, computer equipment

8360 Maintenance, computer software

8400–8490 Vehicles, Travel, and Entertainment

8410 Lease, administrative vehicles

8420 Mileage reimbursement

8430 Repairs and maintenance, administration vehicles

8440 Operating expense, administration vehicles

8450 Taxes, licenses, and insurance, administration vehicles

8460 Travel

8470 Customer business expense

8480 Meeting expenses

8490 In-house meeting expenses

8500–8590 Taxes

8510 Sales-and-use taxes

8520 Real estate taxes

8530 Personal property taxes

8540 License fees

8590 Other taxes

8600–8690 Insurance

8610 Hazard insurance/property insurance

8630 General liability insurance

8690 Other insurance

8700–8790 Professional Services

8710 Accounting services

8720 Legal services

8730 Consulting services

8770 Recruiting and hiring

8790 Other professional expenses

8800–8890 Depreciation Expenses

8810 Depreciation, buildings

8830   Depreciation, vehicles
8840   Depreciation, furniture, and equipment
8860   Amortization of leasehold improvement
8870   Depreciation computer equipment and software
8880   Amortization of organization cost
8890   Depreciation, other
8900–8990   General and Administrative Expense, Other
8900   Bad debts
8910   Contributions
8911   Contributions, political
8920   Dues and subscriptions
8950   Bank charges

8960   Penalties
8990   Training and education expenses
9000–9990   Other Income and Expenses
9100–9190   Other Income
9100   Income from partnerships, joint ventures, S-corps, and LLCs
9150   Gain or loss on sale of assets
9190   Other
9200–9290   Other Expenses
9200   Extraordinary Expenses
9300–9390   Provision for Income Taxes
9300   Provision for federal income taxes
9320   Provision for state income taxes
9330   Provision for local income taxes

Part B. The Complete NAHB Chart of Accounts

1000–1990 Assets

1000–1090 Cash

1010   Petty Cash—All of a company's petty cash accounts, whether maintained in an office or by the construction superintendent in the field.

1020   Cash on Deposit, General—Demand deposits in the bank for all regular trade receipts and disbursements.

1030   Cash on Deposit, Payroll—Demand deposits in the bank for payroll disbursements only. Generally, companies that employ their own crews and write a large number of payroll checks maintain a separate checking account to cover payroll. For each pay period, a check for the total amount of the payroll is written against the general account and deposited in the payroll account.

1040   Cash on Deposit, Savings and Money Market—Deposits in savings and money market accounts.

1050   Cash on Deposit, Held in Escrow—Cash held at title companies, with disbursing agents, and at financial institutions representing refundable customer deposits, completion escrows, or other escrowed funds.

1100–1190   Short-term Investments

1110   Certificates of Deposit—Funds deposited in interest-bearing Certificates of Deposit (CDs) maturing in less than 1 year.

1120   Marketable Securities—Funds invested in readily marketable stock of unaffiliated companies that management intends to dispose of within 1 year. In accordance with generally accepted accounting principles, these investments should be carried at the lower of aggregate cost or market value. To adjust, credit this account and debit 2940 (Unrealized holding loss).

1130   Government Securities—Funds invested in securities issued by federal, state, or local authorities maturing in less than 1 year.

1190   Other Short-term Investments—Funds invested in other instruments for set periods (usually less than 1 year) that earn interest or dividend income.

1200–1290   Receivables

1210   Accounts Receivable, Trade—Amounts due to the business for construction, including customers' orders for extras, management services, or other services performed on open account.

1220   Accounts Receivable, Other—Amounts due to the business for services not otherwise classified.

1230   Notes Receivable—Unpaid balance due to the company on notes received in full or partial settlement of open or short-term accounts.

1250   Mortgage Notes Receivable, Current Year—Mortgages taken from purchasers in lieu of cash. Payments due within 12 months.

1260   Due on Construction and Development Loans—Amounts due from financial institutions on construction and development loans. The balance on this account represents the amount of cash available from construction and development loans. When a loan is approved, debit this account to show how much cash is available through the loan, and credit Account 2220 (Acquisitions, development, and construction loans payable). As you draw cash from the loan, you decrease or credit Account 1260 (Due on construction and development loans) to show how much cash is left to draw from the loan. As an alternative, you can record draws against construction loans directly to account 2220 (Acquisitions, development, and construction loans payable).

1265   Costs in Excess of Billings—This account is used mostly by remodelers, custom builders, and commercial builders to record costs that exceed their estimated costs (sometimes referred to as underbilling) based on the percentage of completion method.

1270   Accrued Interest Receivable—Interest earned but not received from all sources such as bonds, notes, and mortgages.

1280 Allowance for Doubtful Accounts—A contra account that has a credit balance reflecting the potential uncollectable amounts of any account in the receivables classification. A contra account serves the purpose of reducing the balance of an account (in this case, accounts receivable) without changing the account itself.

1290   Retentions   (Retainage)   Receivable—Amounts withheld by customers on progress billings. When retentions become due, Account 1210 (Accounts receivable, trade) is credited while Account 2210 (Accounts payable, trade) is debited.

1300–1390   Inventories

1310   Construction Materials Inventory—Control account for book value of construction materials purchased and stored rather than delivered directly to a job in progress. As materials are allocated to a specific job, the cost is transferred and debited to Account 1430 (Direct construction cost) and credited to Account 1310 (Construction materials inventory). Excess materials purchased directly for a specific job and originally debited to Account 1430 should be debited to Account 1310 and credited to Account 1430, if the materials are transferred to inventory, or they should be allocated to the cost of the house for which the materials are used.

1320   Land Held for Development—Control account for cost of land purchased for future development. The cost of land increases by recording fees, legal fees, and other acquisition costs. Debit the cost of land to Account 1410 (Land and land development) at the time land is to be developed, and credit Account 1320 (Land held for development).

1330   Property Held for Remodeling—Acquisition costs for properties held for future improvement or remodeling. Once the work is completed, they may be sold or held for investment.

1400–1490 Work in Progress

1410 Land and Land Development—Control account for all land and land development costs (see Part F below). Cumulative cost of land and land development, including cost of raw land, financing and interest, land planning, engineering, grading, streets, curb and gutters, sidewalks, storm sewers, temporary utilities, professional fees, permits, and other costs pertaining to the development of the raw land.

1412 Accumulated Allocations, Land, and Land Development Costs—Accumulated write-offs to cost of sales for land and land development costs. At the time of closing, debit the cost of the lot to the appropriate cost of sales account in the 3500 to 3700 series.

1420 Developed Lots—Cost of lots developed prior to purchase to be used for construction. When a house is closed, debit the cost to the appropriate cost of sales account in the 3500 to 3700 series.

1430 Direct Construction Cost—Control account for all direct construction costs (see Part D), including permits, direct labor, materials, subcontractors, equipment rentals, and any other direct charge to the units under construction. This account must be supported by job cost subsidiaries that detail the cost of each construction unit. Also included are finance and interest charges during construction. Never include in this account marketing costs or indirect construction costs. When a house is closed, debit the cost to the appropriate cost of sales account in the 3500 to 3700 series.

1440 Indirect Construction Cost—A control account that requires a detailed breakdown in a subsidiary ledger of the different elements of cost. By adding an additional two digits to establish sub-accounts, a detailed breakdown of the indirect construction costs can be accommodated in the general chart of accounts (see Part E). Indirect construction costs are necessary costs of building that cannot be directly, easily, or economically attributed to a specific house or job. These costs are classified as assets—part of the value of inventories—because they contribute to the value of the work in progress. The Internal Revenue Service and GAAP (generally accepted accounting principles) generally require that real estate and construction inventories include the proportional share of indirect costs. When a house is closed, debit the proportional share of the cost in the 3500 to 3700

series. An alternative method of treating indirect costs is to record the cost within the 4000 series, an operating expense classification. To comply with IRS and GAAP requirements when using the alternative method, allocate the proportional share of indirect construction costs to work in process inventories.

1500–1590 Finished Units and Other Inventory

1510 Finished Units—Accumulated direct and indirect construction costs of units completed but not sold. Transfer from and credit Accounts 1430 (Direct construction cost) and 1440 (Indirect construction cost) at the time of completion. The cost of the lot, accumulated in Account 1420 (Developed lots), is transferred to the 3500–3700 series at the time the sale is closed.

1520 Model Homes—Cost includes lot cost and direct and indirect construction costs used for models. Upon completion of the model, transfer and debit costs to this account from Accounts 1420 (Developed lots), 1430 (Direct construction cost), and 1440 (Indirect construction cost), which are credited. Upon sale of the model, transfer and debit costs to the 3500–3700 series.

1530 Trade-ins and Repossessions—The cost of any trade-ins acquired during a sales transaction and that are held for resale but not held as investment (including refurbishing until sold). Transfer cost to Account 3660 (Cost of sales, trade-ins) when you sell the units.

1600–1690 Other Current Assets

1610 Refundable Deposits—Deposits paid to and held by municipalities, utilities, and other businesses for performance or completion of operation. Also includes refundable plan deposits.

1620 Prepaid Expenses—Unexpired portions of expenses applicable to future periods for items such as insurance, rent, commitment fees, interest, and taxes. Detailed accounts for prepayments may be provided by adding an additional sub-ledger or a two-digit sub-class to the main account number.

1630 Employee Advances—Debit for a salary advance and credit when advance is deducted from payroll or repaid by employee.

1650 Due from Affiliates or Subsidiaries—Short-term receivables due from affiliates or subsidiary companies.

1660 Due from Officers, Stockholders, Owners, or Partners—Amounts currently due from officers, stockholders, owners, or partners of the business.

1690 Other Current Assets—Miscellaneous current assets not otherwise classified.

1700–1790 Investments and Other Assets

1710 Investments, Long-term—Stocks, bonds, and other securities to be held as long-term investments. By using an additional sub-ledger or two-digit sub-class, each type of investment can be maintained in a separate account.

1720 Cash Surrender Value of Officers' Life Insurance—Accumulated net cash surrender value net of any outstanding loans on life insurance carried on officers of the business.

1730 Investments in Affiliated Entities—Capital stock of affiliated companies, subsidiaries, partnerships, and joint ventures. Your company's portion of the equity or loss generated by the affiliated entity should be debited (income) or credited (loss) to this account on a periodic basis with the offsetting entry debited or credited to Account 9100 (Income from partnerships, joint ventures, S-corps, and LLCs), provided that the investing company can exercise significant influence (usually more than 20 percent of the voting power) over the operations of the affiliated entity.

1750 Mortgage Notes Receivable, Long-term—Amounts of mortgages that are due beyond the end of the next fiscal year end.

1760 Due from Affiliated Companies or Subsidiaries, Long-term—Amounts due from affiliated companies or subsidiaries that are to be carried for a long-term period.

1770 Due from Officers, Owners, and Stockholders, Long-term—Amounts due from company officers, owners, and stockholders to be carried for a long-term period. The amount may be an interest-bearing note or an open account.

1780 Organization Cost—Legal fees, corporate charter fees, and other organization costs that are normally capitalized. Amortization of these fees should be credited directly to this account.

1800–1890 Property, Plant, and Equipment

1810 Land—Cost of land acquired for the purpose of constructing company offices and warehouses and/or held for investment. Land held for future development should be included in Account 1320 (Land held for development).

1820 Buildings—Costs relating to offices, warehouses, field offices, field warehouse, and other company structures used in the operation of the business.

1825 Rental Property—Cost of property owned and managed by the company held for investment. Buildings used in the operation of the business should be classified in Account 1820 (Buildings).

1827 Recreation Amenities—Property that the company will retain for ownership and operation. Includes property to be turned over to homeowners' associations in Account 1430 (Direct construction cost).

1830 Office Furniture and Equipment—Cost of office furniture, fixtures, and small equipment used by administrative and office personnel.

1840 Vehicles—Cost of automobiles and trucks owned by the business.

1850 Construction Equipment—The cost of all construction equipment, excluding licensed motor vehicles. Charge or debit small tools of nominal value to Account 1440 (Indirect construction cost) or Account 4560 (Small tools and supplies).

1870 Model Home Furnishings—Cost of model home furniture and furnishings.

1880 Leasehold Improvements—Cost of improvements made to leased property.

1890 Computer Equipment and Software—Cost of computer hardware and software. May be segregated to improve tracking.

1900–1999 Accumulated Depreciation

1920 Accumulated Depreciation, Buildings—Accumulated depreciation on assets carried in Account 1820 (Buildings).

1925 Accumulated Depreciation, Rental Properties—Accumulated depreciation on rental properties carried in Account 1825 (Rental property).

1927 Accumulated Depreciation, Recreation Amenities—Accumulated depreciation on property carried in Account 1827 (Recreations amenities).

1930 Accumulated Depreciation, Office Furniture and Equipment—Accumulated depreciation on assets in Account 1830 (Office furniture and equipment).

1940 Accumulated Depreciation, Vehicles—Accumulated depreciation on assets carried in Account 1840 (Vehicles).

1950 Accumulated Depreciation, Construction Equipment—Accumulated depreciation on assets carried in Account 1850 (Construction equipment).

1970 Accumulated Depreciation, Model Home Furnishings—Accumulated depreciation on assets carried in Account 1870 (Model home property furnishings).

1980 Accumulated Depreciation, Leasehold Improvements—Accumulated depreciation on assets in Account 1880 (Leasehold improvements).

1990 Accumulated Depreciation, Computer Equipment and Software—Accumulated depreciation on assets in Account 1890 (Computer equipment and software).

2000–2990 Liabilities and Owners' Equity

2000–2090 Deposits by Customers

2010 Contract Deposits—Down payments, earnest money, and deposits on contracts. Transfer and credit the deposit to the appropriate account in the 3000–3490 series (Sales and Revenues) when the sale is closed and debit Account 2010 (Contract deposits).

2030 Tenant Security Deposit—Refundable tenants' deposits held to secure proper care of unit.

2040 Advance Rent Collected—Rent collected from tenants that relate to a future period. When the rental income is earned, this account is debited, and Account 3200 (Rental property income) is credited.

2100–2190 Accounts Payable

2110 Accounts Payable, Trade—Amounts payable on open account to suppliers and subcontractors.

2120 Retentions Payable—Amounts withheld from subcontractors until final completion and approval of their work.

2190 Accounts Payable, Other—Other short-term open accounts due to nontrade individuals or companies.

2200–2290 Notes Payable

2200 Line of Credit Payable—Outstanding balance on a revolving line of credit.

2220 Acquisition, Development, and Construction Loans Payable—Control account for all loans from lending institutions for acquisition, development, and construction financing. Detailed accounts for each acquisition, development, and construction

loans payable may be provided by using an additional sub-ledger or a two-digit sub-class to the main account number.

2240 Current Portion of Long-term Debt—Portion of principal payments included in Account 2510 (Long-term notes payable) that are due on notes to be paid within 1 year.

2290 Notes Payable, Other—Notes payable to banks, other financial institutions, and other individuals that are due within 1 year.

2300–2490 Other Current Liabilities

2310 Social Security and Medicare Withheld and Accrued—Accumulated amounts of social security (FICA) and Medicare taxes withheld from employees payroll. This account is also used to accrue the employer's portion of these taxes.

2320 Federal Payroll Tax Withheld—Accumulated amounts of federal taxes withheld from employees' pay and owed to the federal government.

2330 State and Local Payroll Tax Withheld—Accumulated amounts of state taxes withheld from employees' pay and owed to state government. Credit funds withheld from employees' pay, and debit payments to the state income tax division. Also include disability and other state withholding taxes. For multiple states, cities, or other local government withholdings, you may want to set up a separate account or use a two-digit sub-account.

2340 Other Payroll Withholdings—Other accumulated amounts withheld from employees' pay, such as employees' share of health insurance program. Credit funds withheld from employees' pay, and debit payments to the proper agencies.

2345 Union Withholding and Benefits Payable—Accumulated amounts withheld from employees' pay in accordance with a collective bargaining agreement. This account can also be used to accrue the employer's liability for union benefits such as pension and welfare, training, health insurance, and other required benefits. To accrue benefits, credit this account and debit Account 4150 (Union benefits). Debit this account for payments to the union or appropriate fund.

2350 Sales and Use Tax Payable—Credit amount of tax received from purchasers, and debit payments to the taxing authority. Note: Taxes paid on material used in construction are debited to Account 1430 (Direct construction cost) or Account 3830 (Building materials).

2360 Real Estate Taxes Payable—Credit the company's liability incurred to date, and debit payments to the taxing authority.

2370 Income Taxes Payable—Credit for accrual of the company's current liability for federal and state income and franchise taxes, and debit payments to the taxing authorities.

2390 Accrued Interest Payable—Credit interest accrued and payable, and debit payments.

2400 Accrued Salaries and Wages Payable—Control account for accrued salaries and wages. Credit accrued salaries and wages, and debit when payments are made.

2410 Accrued Commissions Payable—Commissions earned but not yet paid. Credit amount of commission due and debit payments.

2420 Workers' Compensation Insurance Payable—Amounts withheld from payment to subcontractors for Workers' Compensation insurance but not yet paid. This account can also be used to accrue the employer's liability for Workers' Compensation on their employees.

2425 Other Accrued Expenses—The liability for expenses that have been incurred but the invoices have not been received or the expense has not been paid, such as professional fees, bonuses, commissions, and vacations. Detailed accounts for other accrued expenses may be provided by adding an additional sub-ledger or a two-digit sub-class to the main account number.

2430 Deferred Income—Advance payments made by tenants or other sources for which income is not yet earned. Credit this account when an advance payment is received. Debit the account when the revenue is earned and credit the appropriate income account.

2440 Due to Affiliated Companies or Subsidiaries—Amounts due to affiliated or subsidiary companies currently due.

2450 Due to Officers, Stockholders, Owners—Amounts due to officers, stockholders, owners, and partners currently due.

2480 Billings in Excess of Costs—This account is used mostly by remodelers, custom builders, and commercial builders to record charges that exceed their estimated costs (sometimes referred to as over-billing) using the percentage of completion method of accounting.

2490 Other Current Liabilities—Miscellaneous current liabilities not otherwise classified.

2500–2890 Long-term Payable Liabilities

2510 Long-term Notes Payable—Control account for notes on vehicles, equipment, and other assets used in operations. Include current portion in Account 2240 (Current portion of long-term debt). Detailed accounts for long-term payable liabilities may be provided by adding an additional sub-ledger or a two-digit sub-class to the main account number.

2530 Mortgage Notes Payable—Control account for mortgages on rental property and land and on buildings used in operations. Include current portion in Account 2240 (Current portion of long-term Debt). Detailed accounts for mortgage notes payable may be provided by adding an additional sub-ledger or a two-digit sub-class to the main account number.

2600 Deferred Income Taxes Payable—Income taxes due on deferred income.

2610 Due to Affiliated Companies or Subsidiaries, Long-term—Amounts due to affiliated companies or subsidiaries that are to be carried for a long-term period.

2620 Due to Officers, Stockholders, Owners, Long-term, and Partners—Amounts due to company officers, stockholders, owners, and partners to be carried for a long-term period of time.

2700 Other Long-term Liabilities—Long-term liabilities not otherwise classified.

2900–2990 Owners' Equity

2900 Common Stock—Par value or stated value of stock outstanding.

2910 Additional Paid in Capital—Amounts received in excess of par or stated value of stock.

2920 Retained Earnings—Prior years' accumulation of profits.

2930 Treasury Stock—The corporation's own capital stock that has been issued and then reacquired by the corporation by either purchase or gift.

2940 Unrealized Holding Loss—Represents cumulative unrealized loss on investments or marketable securities. Investments or marketable securities should be adjusted to their market values on an annual or periodic basis.

2950 Partnership or Proprietorship Account—Separate account for each partner, indicating accumulated equity to date. Detailed accounts for Partnership or Proprietorship Account may be provided by adding an additional sub-ledger or a two-digit sub-class to the main account number.

2960 Distributions, Dividends, and Draws—Accumulated owners' withdrawals for period. Maintain a separate account for each owner. At the end of the fiscal year, the account should be closed and amounts transferred and debited to Account 2920 (Retained earnings) or 2950 (Partnership or proprietorship account) as applicable. Detailed accounts for Distributions, Dividends, and Draws may be provided by adding an additional sub-ledger or a two-digit sub-class to the main account number.

3000–3990 Sales, Revenues, and Cost of Sales
3000–3490 Sales and Revenues
3000 Sales, Land Held for Development—Revenues earned from sales of raw land not yet subdivided and without improvements.
3050 Sales, Developed Lots—Revenues earned from sales of partially or fully developed lots.
3100 Sales, Single-Family Speculative—Revenues earned from sales of spec houses.
3110 Sales, Single-Family Production—Revenues earned from sales of production houses.
3120 Sales, Single-Family Custom Designed—Revenues earned from sales of custom houses.
3125 Sales, Single-Family Custom, No Land—Revenues earned from sales of houses built under contract on land owned by someone other than the builder.
3130 Sales, Residential Remodeling—Revenues earned from sales of residential remodeling work.
3133 Sales, Commercial and Industrial Remodeling—Revenues earned from sales of commercial and industrial remodeling work.
3135 Sales, Insurance Restoration—Revenues earned from sales of insurance restoration work.
3137 Sales, Repairs—Revenues earned from sales of repair work.
3140 Sales, Multifamily—Revenues earned from sales of multifamily units.
3150 Sales, Commercial and Industrial—Revenues earned from sales of new commercial and industrial construction.
3160 Sales, Trade-ins, and Repossessions—Revenues earned from sales of houses originally received as partial payment on another sale or repossessed.
3190 Sales, Other—Revenues earned from sales of construction activities not otherwise classified.
3200 Rental Property Income—Revenues earned from rental of investment property and office space.

3210 Common Area Reimbursements—Revenues earned from tenant reimbursement of common area expenses. Common area expenses should be charged to the applicable account within the 7000 series. Other reimbursements should be credited to Account 3220 (Other reimbursements).
3220 Other Reimbursements—Revenues earned from tenant reimbursement of expenses. Expenses incurred by the company should be charged to the applicable account within the 7000 series.
3230 Parking Fee Income—Revenue earned from sales of the rental of company-owned parking facilities.
3240 Amenities Facilities Income—Revenue earned from rental and use charges for company-owned recreational facilities.
3360 Construction Management Fee Income—Revenues earned from construction management activities.
3379 Design Fee Income—Revenues earned from design activities.
3400 Miscellaneous Income—Revenues earned from sources not otherwise classified.
3410 Interest Income—Interest earned from Certificates of Deposits, savings accounts, and other sources.
3420 Dividend Income—Dividends earned from investments in stocks, bonds, and other sources.
3450 Earned Discounts—Cash discounts earned from payment on account within the time established by the supplier or subcontractor.
3490 Sales Concessions and Discounts—This account records the difference between the published sales price and the contract price. It is used to capture the impact of concessions on company margins. If this account is used, then the published price is placed in the appropriate sales account, and concessions and discounts are debited here. This is a contra account and thus a reduction to sales.

3500–3700 Cost of Sales
3500 Cost of Sales, Land Held for Development—Transfer from and credit Account 1320 (Land held for development) at the time of sale and debit Account 3500 (Cost of sales, land held for development).
3550 Cost of Sales, Developed Lots—Allocated amount to be written off on lots sold. Credit Account 1420, if the lot was developed prior to pur-

chase, or 1412 (Accumulated allocations, land and land development costs) if the company developed the lot, and debit Account 3550 (Cost of sales, developed lots).

3600 Cost of Sales, Single-Family Speculative— Direct construction costs related to sales of homes recorded in Account 3100 (Cost of sales, single-family speculative). Transfer from and credit Account 1430 (Direct construction cost). Debit Account 3600.

3610 Cost of Sales, Single-Family Production— Direct construction costs of houses built under contract. Transfer from Account 1430 (Direct construction cost). Debit Account 3610 (Cost of sales, single-family production).

3620 Cost of Sales, Single-Family Custom Designed—Direct construction costs of custom houses. Transfer from Account 1430 (Direct construction cost) if applicable. Debit Account 3620 (Cost of sales, single-family custom designed).

3625 Cost of Sales, Single Family Custom, No Land—Direct construction costs of custom homes built on land owned by someone other than the builder. Transfer from 1430 (Direct construction cost) if applicable. Debit Account 3625 (Cost of sales, single-family custom, no land).

3630 Cost of Sales, Remodeling—Direct construction costs of remodeling. Transfer from Account 1430 (Direct construction cost) if applicable. Debit Account 3630 (Cost of sales, remodeling). An alternative method is to use 3800 account series for directly posting remodeling costs to costs of sales.

3633 Cost of Sales, Commercial and Industrial Remodeling—Direct construction costs of commercial and industrial jobs. Transfer from Account 1430 (Direct construction cost) if applicable. Debit Account 3633 (Cost of sales, commercial and industrial remodeling).

3635 Cost of Sales, Insurance Restoration— Direct costs for insurance restoration work. Transfer from Account 1430 (Direct construction cost) if applicable. Debit Account 3635.

3637 Cost of Sales, Repairs—Direct costs for repairs. Transfer from Account 1430 (Direct construction cost) if applicable. Debit Account 3637 (Cost of sales, insurance restoration).

3640 Cost of Sales, Multifamily—Direct construction costs of multifamily units sold. Transfer from Account 1430 (Direct construction cost). Debit Account 3640(Cost of sales, multifamily).

3650 Cost of Sales, Commercial and Industrial—Direct construction costs of commercial and industrial jobs. Transfer from Account 1430 (Direct construction cost) if applicable. Debit Account 3650 (Cost of sales, commercial and industrial).

3660 Cost of Sales, Trade-ins—Trade-in allowance and refurbishing. Transfer from Account 1530 (Trade-ins and repossessions) at time of sale. Debit Account 3660 (Cost of sales, trade-ins).

3690 Cost of Sales, Other—Costs incurred to generate income from sources not otherwise classified.

3700 Direct Construction Cost for Prior Periods—Cost adjustments to cost of sales for charges or credits from prior periods closings. These adjustments are for changes in cost that have not been accounted for after closing of an individual unit.

3800–3899 Costs of Construction

The following accounts can be used by remodelers and builders for direct posting of construction costs to cost of sales instead of posting direct construction costs to Account 1430 (Direct Construction Cost).

3810 Direct Labor—Include the gross wages paid to lead carpenters and crews engaged in the remodeling process.

3820 Labor Burden—Payroll taxes and workers compensation insurance as well as other items such as health insurance and life and disability insurance that relate to gross wages paid to the field crew. Also include vacation, holiday, sick, and other paid days off for the field crew.

3830 Building Material—Cost of materials used on a remodeling project. Include all freight and taxes paid on the material in this account.

3840 Subcontractors—Cost of subcontractors used on a specific remodeling project.

3850 Rental Equipment—Cost of rental equipment used on a specific remodeling project.

3860 Other Direct Costs—Include costs of small tools consumed on a specific remodeling project, cost of permits and fees obtained for a particular project, and any other direct construction costs not otherwise classified.

3870 Professional Design Fees—Costs paid to architects, engineers, and interior designers, certified kitchen designers and bath designers for use on a specific remodeling job. Also include in-house design salaries, wages, and the related labor burden in this account if they are incurred on a specific remodeling job.

4000–4990 Indirect Construction Cost

The 4000 series of accounts is an alternative to Account 1440 (Indirect construction cost). The 4000 series allows a detailed breakdown of accounts in the general ledger, while maintaining a four-digit numerical code. The indirect costs accumulated in these accounts must still be allocated to houses or specific jobs held in inventory to comply with generally accepted accounting principles and/or IRS regulations.

4000–4090 Salaries and Wages

Salaries and wages of personnel directly engaged in the construction process but not identified with a specific unit.

4010 Superintendents—Salaries of supervisory personnel for time spent in organizing, planning, or supervising production crews. This category does not include wages of personnel who work on specific jobs with their crews.

4020 Laborers—Wages paid to laborers on construction that cannot be charged to a specific job. Labor should be estimated, budgeted, and charged to a specific job if possible.

4030 Project and Production Manager—Salaries paid to supervisors of superintendents.

4040 Architects, Drafters, Estimators, and Purchasers—Salaries and wages of persons who perform these duties for construction jobs. If the area is department to itself, each person's job may be broken down into a separate account.

4050 Warranty and Customer Service Manager—Salaries of employees responsible for the warranty and service function.

4060 Warranty and Customer Service Wages—Labor incurred to repair, replace, or service any item after possession by owner on a particular unit.

4070 Other Indirect Construction Wages—Salaries and wages of personnel, such as timekeepers, security guards, and/or quality control inspectors involved in the construction process but not identified with specific units.

4100–4190 Payroll Taxes and Benefits

4110 Payroll Taxes—Accumulated share of FICA, unemployment, Medicare, social security, and other company-paid taxes relating to salaries and wages charged as indirect cost.

4120 Workers' Compensation Insurance—Insurance premiums for individual construction workers.

4130 Health and Accident Insurance—Premiums for health and accident insurance for indirect construction workers.

4140 Retirement, Pension, and Profit Sharing—Employer contributions to retirement, pension, and profit-sharing plans for indirect construction workers.

4150 Union Benefits—Benefits related to indirect construction workers in accordance with a collective bargaining agreement.

4190 Other Benefits—Benefits relating to salaries and wages charged as indirect costs not otherwise classified.

4200–4290 Field Office Expenses

Maintenance and repairs, utilities, telephone, and other expenses incidental to a field office, including erection and moving. The field office is often a trailer. If the office is in a model, include these expenses in 6600 accounts (Model Home Expenses).

4210 Rent, Field Office—Rent of a field office.

4230 Repairs and Maintenance, Field Office—Repairs and maintenance, including service contracts, of a field office.

4250 Utilities, Field Office—Heat, electricity, and other utilities for a field office.

4260 Telephone, Field Office—Installation and monthly charges for field office telephones and related communications equipment.

4265 Mobile Phones, Pagers, and Radios—Purchase and monthly charges for cellular phones, pagers, and field radios for construction personnel.

4290 Other Field Office Expenses—Other expenses for a field office not included in other categories.

4300–4390 Warehouse and Storage Expense

Costs incurred in material handling and storage if materials are not delivered to the job site by the supplier.

4310 Rent, Warehouse and Storage—Rent on warehouse and storage facilities.

4330 Repairs and Maintenance, Warehouse and Storage—Repairs and maintenance, including service contracts, of warehouse and storage facilities.

4350 Utilities, Warehouse and Storage—Heat, electricity, and other utilities for warehouse and storage facilities.

4360 Telephone, Warehouse and Storage—Installation of and monthly charges for telephone in warehouse and storage.

4400–4490 Construction Vehicles, Travel, and Entertainment

4410 Lease Payments, Construction Vehicles—Payments on leased or rented vehicles used by construction personnel.

4420 Mileage Reimbursement—Payment to field personnel for use of their private vehicles.

4430 Repairs and Maintenance, Construction Vehicles—Repair and maintenance costs for automobiles and trucks used by construction personnel, including minor repairs and major overhauls.

4440 Operating Expenses, Construction Vehicles—Fuel, oil, and lubrication expenses for automobiles and trucks used by construction personnel.

4450 Taxes, Licenses, Insurance, Construction Vehicles—Property damage and liability insurance, licenses, fees, and taxes on vehicles used by construction personnel.

4460 Travel, Construction Department—Travel expense incurred by construction personnel.

4470 Customer Business Entertainment, Construction—Business-related entertainment expenses incurred by construction personnel.

4480 Training and Education, Construction—Training and education expenses incurred by construction personnel.

4490 Recruiting Fees and Expenses, Construction Personnel—Expenses associated with the hiring of construction personnel.

4500–4590 Construction Equipment—Costs of maintaining and operating construction equipment.

4510 Rent, Construction Equipment—Payments on leased or rented equipment.

4530 Repairs and Maintenance, Construction Equipment—Repair and maintenance costs on equipment.

4540 Operating Expenses, Construction Equipment—Fuel, oil, and lubrication expenses on equipment.

4550 Taxes and Insurance, Construction Equipment—Taxes and insurance required on equipment.

4560 Small Tools and Supplies—Cost of items such as hand tools, shovels, skill saws, small power tools, and extension cords used in construction.

4600–4690 Expenses for Maintaining Unsold Units and Units under Construction—Costs applicable to units under construction until delivered to customer.

4610 Temporary Utilities—Utility hook-up costs and utility bills related to units under construction. Custom and small-volume builders may consider classifying these costs as part of direct construction costs.

4620 Trash Maintenance—Cost of trash hauling, dumpsters, and other equipment to maintain construction site.

4640 Lawn Care—Costs required to maintain the lawn prior to transfer to customer.

4650 Utilities, Completed Units—Utility cost and hook-ups for finished units held in inventory and awaiting sale.

4660 Repairs and Maintenance, Completed Units—Cost of repair and maintenance to any unit held in inventory for sale.

4700–4790 Warranty and Customer Service

4710 Salaries and Wages, Warranty—Labor incurred to repair, replace, or service any item after possession by owner on a particular unit.

4720 Materials, Warranty—Price of materials to repair, replace, or service any item after possession by owner on a particular unit.

4730 Subcontractor, Warranty—Cost of subcontractor incurred to repair, replace, or service any item after possession by owner on a particular unit.

4790 Other Warranty Expenses—Costs other than labor, materials, or subcontractors incurred to repair, replace, or service any item after possession by owner on a particular unit.

4800–4890 Depreciation Expenses

4820 Depreciation, Construction Office—Depreciation on construction office equipment.

4830 Depreciation, Warehouse—Depreciation of warehouse.

4840 Depreciation, Construction Vehicle—Depreciation expenses of construction vehicles.

4850 Depreciation, Construction Equipment—Depreciation expenses of construction equipment.

4900–4990 Other

4910 Insurance and Bonding Expenses—Cost of obtaining insurance or bonding for construction projects and properties.

4920 Builders Risk Insurance—Cost of obtaining builders risk insurance. Custom and small-volume builders may be more inclined to treat this as a direct cost.

4990 Absorbed Indirect Costs—To comply with IRS and generally accepted accounting principles requirements this is a contra account used to allocate the proportional share of indirect construction costs to work in process inventories. This contra account requires a year-end closing adjustment, which is usually handled by an accountant.

5000–5990 Financing Expenses

5000–5090 Interest

5010 Interest on Line of Credit—Interest expense on loans held by banks and other lenders for operating capital.

5020 Interest on Notes Payable—Interest expense on notes payable for fixed assets such as office buildings and vehicles.

5030 Interest Expense on Developed Lots—Interest expense on developed lots not currently under construction.

5040 Interest Incurred on Construction Loans—Interest expense paid during the building of a house. To comply with IRS and GAAP (generally accepted accounting principles) requirements, interest on construction loans must be capitalized during the period of construction. If interest is posted to this account, to comply with IRS and GAAP requirements, allocate the proportionate share of interest to work in process inventories.

5050 Interest on Completed Inventory—Interest expense paid after completion of construction and before closing of the unit.

5090 Interest Expense, Other—Other interest paid or accrued.

5100–5190 Construction Loan Points and Fees

5120 Points and Fees—Expenses paid on points and fees for construction loans.

5130 Appraisal and Related Fees—Service charges paid for appraisal of property relating to construction loans.

5140 Inspection Fees—Fees for inspection by lenders.

5200–5290 Closing Costs—Closing costs related to the sale of finished houses.

5210 Closing Costs—Closing costs related to the sale of finished houses, usually paid by the seller. Custom and small-volume builders may charge this as a direct expense. If paid on buyer's behalf as a concession, include in Account 6930 (Sales concessions).

5220 Title and Recording—Fees charged for searching and recording, and for title insurance.

5230 Loan Fees—Origination or standby fees on permanent financing commitments.

6000–6990 Sales and Marketing Expenses

This section of the operating expense chart of accounts is reserved for sales and marketing expenses that may be written off as period expenses.

6000– 6090 Sales Salaries and Commissions

6010 Sales Manager's Compensation—Compensation, including bonuses or incentives, for sales managers.

6030 Salaries, Sales Personnel—Salaries for noncommission activities, excluding draws against present or future commissions.

6040 Sales Commissions, In-house—Commissions paid to employees. Remodelers sometimes charge this as a direct cost.

6050 Sales Commissions, Outside—Commissions paid to sales agents and others not employed by the company.

6090 Other Sales Office Salaries—Salaries and wages for clerical and other personnel who work directly for the sales department or sales office.

6100–6190 Payroll Taxes and Benefits, Sales and Marketing—Payroll taxes and benefits associated with Salaries and wages of the sales and marketing department or sales office employees.

6110 Payroll Taxes, Sales and Marketing—Accumulated share of FICA, unemployment, and other taxes relating to salaries and wages of sales and marketing personnel.

6120 Workers' Compensation Insurance, Sales and Marketing—Insurance premiums on salaries and wages of sales and marketing personnel.

6130 Health and Accident Insurance, Sales and Marketing—Premiums for health and accident insurance for sales and marketing personnel.

6140 Retirement, Pension, and Profit-Sharing Plans, Sales and Marketing—Employer contributions paid to retirement, pension, and profit-sharing plans for sales and marketing personnel.

6190 Other Benefits—Benefits relating to salaries and wages of sales and marketing personnel.

6200–6290 Sales Office Expenses—Operating costs relating to a separate sales office or design center. If the sales office is in a model, include expenses in the 6660–6690 account series (Model Home Maintenance).

6210 Rent, Sales Office—Rental of sales office.

6230 Repairs and Maintenance, Sales Office—Cost of all interior and exterior sales office building repairs and maintenance, including interior remodeling not capitalized, janitorial service, landscaping, and window washing.

6250 Utilities, Sales Office—Heat and other utilities for the sales office.

6260 Telephone, Sales Office—Installation of and monthly charges for the sales office, both landline and cell phones.

6270 Supplies, Sales Office—Office supplies used by sales office staff.

6300–6390 Advertising and Sales Promotion

6310 Print Advertising—Classified and display advertising expenses.

6320 Radio Advertising—Expenses for radio time and related services.

6325 Television Advertising—Expenses for television time and related services.

6330 Internet Fees, Web Page Design, and Maintenance Costs—Expenses for Internet fees, design of world wide web pages, and related maintenance fees.

6340 Brochures and Catalogues—Cost of designing and printing brochures and catalogues.

6350 Signs—Photography, typography, printing, artwork, copy writing, materials, and supply expenses required to make signs.

6355 Billboards—Fees paid for art and advertising on billboards.

6365 Promotions—Fees paid for special programs—i.e., move-in gifts.

6370 Agency Commissions—Fees paid to agencies that assist in setting up advertising programs.

6380 Multiple Listing Fees—Payments to a centralized brokerage service.

6390 Public Relations—Fees paid to public relations firms for press releases and other publicity.

6395 Referral Fees—Payments for referrals.

6400–6490 Sales Vehicles, Travel, and Entertainment

6410 Lease Payment, Sales Vehicles—Payments on leased or rented vehicles used for sales and marketing personnel.

6420 Mileage Reimbursement, Sales and Marketing—Payment to sales and marketing personnel for use of their private vehicles.

6430 Repairs and Maintenance, Sales Vehicles—Repair and maintenance costs of the company's automobiles used by sales and marketing personnel, including minor repairs and major overhauls.

6440 Operating Expense, Sales and Marketing Vehicles—Fuel, oil, and lubrication costs.

6450 Taxes, Licenses, Insurance, Sales and Marketing Vehicles—Property damage and liability insurance, licenses, fees, and taxes on the company's vehicles used by sales and marketing personnel.

6460 Travel, Sales and Marketing—Travel expenses incurred by sales and marketing personnel.

6470 Customer Business Entertainment, Sales and Marketing—Entertainment expenses incurred by sales and marketing personnel.

6600–6690 Model Home Maintenance

6610 Rent or Lease Payments, Model Home Furnishings—Costs of renting or leasing model home furnishings.

6620 Rent or Lease Payments, Model Home—Costs of renting or leasing a model home.

6625 Decorating Fees, Model Home—Fee for decorating services.

6630 Repairs and Maintenance, Model Homes—Repairs maintenance and decoration expenses resulting from use, damage, or minor changes to the model or its furnishings.

6650 Utilities, Model Homes—Heat, electricity, water, and sewer expenses.

6670 Lawn and Landscaping Care, Model Homes—Labor and material costs for lawn cutting and for watering, seeding, fertilizing, and pruning lawn and other plantings.

6680 Cleanup, Model Homes—Costs relating to window washing and daily cleanup.

6690 Interest on Model Homes—Interest paid after completion of the model home(s).

6700–6790 Sales and Marketing Fees

6710 Market Research and Consultation— Fees for market research and consultation.

6720 Interior Design Fee—Fees paid for outside designer to assist buyers with their selections.

6770 Recruiting Fees and Expenses, Sales and Marketing Personnel—Expenses associated with the hiring of sales and marketing personnel.

6780 Training and Education Expenses—Cost of travel, registration fees for seminars and conventions, hotel and lodging expenses, in-house programs, literature, and materials. Also include expenses incurred for conventions and trade shows as well as national, state, and local association meetings.

6800–6890 Depreciation

6810 Depreciation, Sales Office—Depreciation on sales office.

6830 Depreciation, Sales Vehicles—Depreciation on sales and marketing vehicles.

6870 Depreciation, Model Home Furnishings and Decorations—Depreciation on model home furnishings and decorations.

6900–6990 Other Marketing Expense

6930 Sales Concessions—Announced discounts, rebates, and other incentives (such as gifts and travel incentives) provided to customers as part of marketing and sales strategy.

6940 Buydowns—Refunds of interest and points issued to customers in the sales process.

6999 Other Sales and Marketing Expenses— Sales and Marketing expenses not otherwise classified.

7000–7990 Operating and Management Expense, Rental Operations

7000–7090 Property Management Salaries and Wages

7010 Property Manager's Compensation—Compensation, including bonuses or incentives, for managers of property management personnel.

7030 Salaries and Wages, Property Management Personnel—Direct salaries and wages for noncommission activities, excluding draws against present and future commissions, which should be debited to Account 7040 (Commissions, in-house) or Account 7050 (Commissions, outside).

7040 Commissions, In-house—Commissions paid to property management personnel employed by the company for leasing of rental property.

7050 Commissions, Outside—Commissions paid to sales agents and others not employed by the company for leasing of rental property.

7060 Salaries and Wages to Maintenance Personnel—Wages and salaries of company personnel assigned to maintenance and repair of rental property. To track different types of work performed by maintenance personnel (i.e., janitorial services, landscaping, repair), you may want to add a one- or two-digit prefix for each type of work performed.

7070 Payroll Taxes and Benefits, Rental Operations—Cost of the company's FICA, Medicare, and federal and state unemployment insurance for rental personnel.

7072 Workers' Compensation Insurance, Rental—Insurance premiums on salaries and wages of rental personnel.

7073 Health and Accident Insurance, Rental— Premiums for health and accident insurance for rental personnel.

7074 Retirement, Pension, and Profit-Sharing Plans, Rental—Employer contributions to retirement, pension, and profit-sharing plans for rental personnel.

7079 Other Benefits Rental—Salaries and wages for in-house clerical and other personnel involved in property management activities not otherwise classified.

7100–7190 Rental Expenses

7110 Advertising—Costs for advertising directly related to renting individual rental units.

7130 Credit Reports—Charges from credit bureaus for reports on prospective tenants.

7190 Other Rental Expenses—Rental expenses not otherwise classified, such as concessions to tenants.

7200–7290 Administrative Expense, Rental Operations

7220 Management and Service Fees—Fees paid to outside firms for the management and operation of a company-owned property management activity.

7230 Office Expenses—Costs for maintaining an office for a property management activity, including rent, supplies, and postage.

7240 Telephone—Costs of the standard monthly charges and long-distance calls directly related to a property management activity.

7250 Tenant Bad Debts—Write-off of past-due rents receivable from tenants.

7260 Collection Costs—Costs incurred in pursuing collection of past-due rents receivable, including collection agency fees.

7290 Other Administrative Expenses—Administrative expenses of a property management activity not otherwise classified.

7300–7390 Professional Services, Rental Operations

7310 Legal Services—Charges for legal counsel for all services relating to a property management activity.

7320 Accounting Services—Charges for preparation of financial statements, tax advice, and other services rendered by an outside accounting firm relating to a property management activity.

7330 Market Research—Charges from consulting firms or individuals for market research relating to a property management activity.

7390 Other Professional Services, Rental Operations—Professional service costs for a property management activity not otherwise classified.

7400–7490 Operating Expense, Rental Operations

7410 Utilities—Gas, electricity, water and sewer service, and other utilities for rental buildings.

7420 Engineering—Payroll and other costs associated with engineering activity related to property management.

7430 Janitorial—Costs for janitorial services for property management activity.

7440 Trash Removal Service—Costs of contracted services for the removal of trash and other waste from related buildings.

7450 Exterminating—Supplies and other costs associated with exterminating services supplied by the company's personnel or an independent contractor.

7460 Snow Removal—Supplies and other costs associated with snow removal services supplied by the company's personnel or an independent contractor.

7470 Other Contractual Services—Costs of services such as sign painting and design provided under contract for a property management activity and not otherwise classified.

7480 Motor Vehicles and Equipment, Rental Operations—Cost of leasing and operating equipment for use at the rental property.

7490 Other Rental Operations Expenses—Operating costs of a rental property not otherwise classified.

7500–7590 Taxes and Insurance, Rental Operations

7510 Real Estate Property Taxes—Local taxes on rental property land, improvements, and buildings.

7520 Personal Property Taxes—Local taxes assessed on business-owned personal property at a rental property.

7530 Franchise Taxes—State tax on rental property for the privilege of doing business.

7540 License Fees—Local fees for licenses, registrations, and permits.

7570 Insurance, Rental Operations—Costs for general liability, property damage, and extended fire insurance.

7590 Other Taxes and Insurance, Rental Operations—Tax and insurance costs not otherwise classified.

7600–7690 Maintenance and Repair Expense, Rental Operations

7610 Tenant Redecorating—Payroll, supplies, and all other costs associated with redecorating rental units, including services supplied by the company's personnel or independent contractors.

7630 Maintenance Contracts and Services—Charges from independent contractors for maintenance and repair services.

7640 Ground Maintenance and Repairs—Costs of maintaining rental property grounds, including landscaping provided by the company's personnel or an independent contractor.

7650 Vehicle Maintenance and Repairs, Rental Operations—Labor and material costs associated with the general maintenance and repair of the company's motor vehicles used at a rental property.

7660 Equipment Maintenance and Repairs, Rental Operations—Labor and materials costs incurred by the company's personnel or an outside contractor for the maintenance and repair of equipment used at a rental property.

7670 Recreational Facilities Maintenance and Repairs—Labor and materials costs incurred by the company's personnel or an outside contractor for the maintenance and repair of recreational facilities at a rental property.

7700–7790   Financing Expenses, Rental Operations

7710 Interest on Mortgage Payable—Interest charges associated with the permanent mortgage loan on rental buildings.

7720 Interest on Notes Payable—Interest charges associated with notes payable associated with rental operations.

7800–7890   Depreciation Expense, Rental Operations

7810 Depreciation, Building—Depreciation for buildings such as rental properties.

7820 Depreciation, Maintenance Equipment—Depreciation for company-owned equipment used for maintaining rental premises.

7830 Depreciation, Vehicles—Depreciation for company-owned vehicles and maintenance equipment used at rental properties.

7840 Depreciation, Furniture and Fixtures—Depreciation for company-owned furniture, fixtures, office machines, and office equipment used for rental operations.

7850 Depreciation, Amenities—Depreciation for rental property recreational facilities.

7890 Other Depreciation—Depreciation for assets not otherwise classified used in rental operations.

7900–7990   Other Management and Operating Expenses—Management and operating expenses not otherwise classified.

8000–8990   General and Administrative Expenses

8000–8090   Salaries, Wages, and Bonuses

8010 Salaries, Owners—Total compensation paid to owners including salaries and bonuses.

8020 Salaries, Officers—Total compensation paid to company officers who are not company owners including salaries and bonuses.

8030 Salaries, Management—Total compensation paid to upper- and middle-management personnel other than owners or officers including salaries and bonuses.

8050 Salaries and Wages, Office and Clerical—Total compensation paid to clerical and other personnel below the managerial level including salaries, wages, and bonuses.

8090 Other General and Administrative Salaries and Wages—Total compensation paid to general and administrative personnel and those not otherwise classified including salaries, wages, and bonuses.

8100–8190   Payroll Taxes and Benefits

8110 Payroll Taxes—Cost of the company's FICA, Medicare, federal and state unemployment insurance, and other local taxes that relate to administrative salaries and wages.

8120 Workers' Compensation Insurance—Insurance premiums for Workers' Compensation paid by the employer for administrative and hourly employees.

8130 Health and Accident Insurance—Health and accident insurance premiums paid by the employer for administrative personnel.

8140 Retirement, Pension, and Profit-Sharing Plans—Employee contributions to retirement, pension, and profit-sharing plans for administrative personnel.

8190 Other Employee Benefits—Benefits relating to salaries and wages of administrative personnel.

8200–8290   Office Expense

8210 Rent—Rental payments for administrative office space.

8220 Office Equipment Rental—Rental payments on office equipment, cellular phones, and pagers for office personnel.

8230 Repairs and Maintenance, Administrative Office Space—Cost of all interior and exterior administrative office building repairs and maintenance, including interior remodeling not capitalized, janitorial service, landscaping, and window washing.

8240 Repairs and Maintenance, Administrative Office Equipment—All contracts and other charges for maintenance of office equipment.

8250 Utilities, Administrative Office—Cost of utilities that serve the administrative offices.

8260 Telephone, Administrative Office—Standard monthly fees and long-distance charges, including cell phones, not applied to other functions or departments.

8270 Office Supplies, Administrative Office—Printing, stationery, and other office supplies.

8280 Postage and Deliveries—Stamps, express mail, couriers, FedEx, UPS, and other delivery services.

8290 Miscellaneous Expenses, Administrative Office—Office expenses not otherwise classified, including answering service monthly fees and paging services.

8300–8390 Computer Expenses

8310 Computer Supplies—Paper, ribbons, and miscellaneous supplies necessary to the operation of the computer system.

8320 Leases, Computer Hardware—Lease payments on leased hardware.

8330 Leases, Computer Software—Lease payments on leased software.

8350 Repairs and Maintenance, Computer Equipment—Service contract or other payments for the maintenance of computer hardware.

8360 Maintenance, Computer Software—Contract or other payments for the maintenance agreement of the systems software.

8400–8490 Vehicle, Travel, and Entertainment

8410 Lease, Administrative Vehicles—Payments on leased or rental vehicles used by administrative personnel.

8420 Mileage Reimbursement—Payments to administrative personnel for use of their private vehicles.

8430 Repairs and Maintenance, Administrative Vehicles—Repair and maintenance costs of automobiles used by administrative personnel, including minor repairs and major overhauls.

8440 Operating Expense, Administrative Vehicles—Vehicle fuel, oil, and lubrication costs.

8450 Taxes, Licenses, and Insurance, Administrative Vehicles—Taxes, licenses, fees, and property damage and liability insurance on vehicles used by administrative personnel.

8460 Travel—Travel expenses incurred by administrative personnel.

8470 Customer Business Expense—Entertainment expenses incurred by administrative personnel.

8480 Meeting Expenses—Expenses incurred by officers and employees representing the company before groups, industry meetings, or other outside events.

8490 In-House Meeting Expenses—Expenses incurred in providing in-house meetings.

8500–8590 Taxes

8510 Sales-and-Use Taxes—Taxes imposed by states, counties, and cities on nondirect construction cost materials used within the city limits but purchased outside those boundaries.

8520 Real Estate Taxes—Tax on property used for the company's offices, and realty taxes not charged elsewhere.

8530 Personal Property Taxes—Assessment of personal property owned by the company.

8540 License Fees—License, registration, municipal fees, and operating permits.

8590 Other Taxes—Taxes not otherwise classified, such as state tax on capitalization and franchise tax.

8600–8690 Insurance

8610 Hazard Insurance/Property Insurance—Fire and extended coverage on buildings and contents.

8630 General Liability Insurance—Costs of liability insurance other than vehicles, including general and product liability insurance.

8690 Other Insurance—Insurance premiums not otherwise classified.

8700–8790 Professional Services

8710 Accounting Services—Audit charges and charges for assistance in the preparation of financial statements, tax advice, and other services rendered by an outside accounting firm.

8720 Legal Services—Charges submitted by legal counsel for services rendered.

8730 Consulting Services—Service bureau, timesharing, or professional fees for services rendered.

8770 Recruiting and Hiring—Expenses associated with hiring administrative personnel.

8790 Other Professional Expenses—Professional fees not otherwise classified.

8800–8890 Depreciation Expenses

8810 Depreciation, Buildings—Depreciation on company buildings such as administrative offices.

8830 Depreciation, Vehicles—Depreciation on company-owned vehicles used by administrative personnel.

8840 Depreciation, Furniture, and Equipment—Depreciation on furniture, fixtures, office machines, and other equipment.

8860 Amortization of Leasehold Improvement—Amortization of improvements to office buildings leased from another entity.

8870 Depreciation, Computer Equipment and Software—Deprecation for computer hardware and software. These may be segregated for easier tracking and control.

8880 Amortization of Organization Cost—Write-off of organization cost, including legal fees and corporate charter fees.

8890 Depreciation, Other—Depreciation and amortization charges not otherwise classified.

8900–8990 General and Administrative Expense, Other

8900 Bad Debts—Charge for uncollectable amounts on receivables. Credit goes to Account 1290, Allowance for doubtful accounts.

8910 Contributions—All charitable donations.

8911 Contributions, Political—All contributions made to political organizations and candidates. These contributions are generally not deductible.

8920 Dues and Subscriptions—Trade association dues and subscriptions for magazines, newspapers, trade journals, business publications, reports, and manuals.

8950 Bank Charges—Bank fees for miscellaneous charges. Check printing should be charged to Account 8270, Office supplies.

8960 Penalties and Other Nondeductible Expenses—Tax penalties, fines, parking tickets.

8990 Training and Education Expenses—Cost of travel, registration fees for seminars and conventions, hotel and lodging expenses, in-house programs, literature, and materials. Also includes expenses incurred for conventions and trade shows as well as national, state, and local association meetings.

9000–9990 Other Income and Expenses

9100–9190 Other Income—Income derived from sources other than the main activity of the business.

9100 Income from Partnerships, Joint Ventures, S-Corps, and LLCs—Income (loss) from participation in partnerships, joint ventures, S-corps, and LLCs.

9150 Gain or Loss on Sale of Assets—Gain or loss (debit) on the sale of assets that had been used in the operation of the business, such as motor vehicles, computers, and office equipment.

9190 Other—Income derived from sources other than the main activity of the business, including speaking and consulting fees, expert witness fees, home inspections, real estate, budgeting fees.

9200–9290 Other Expenses—Extraordinary expenses or expenses attributable to activities not relating to the main activity of the business.

9200 Extraordinary Expenses—Expenses attributable to activities not relating to the main activity of the business. Separate account numbers within this series can be set up to track different categories of other expenses.

9300–9390 Provision for Income Taxes—Provision for federal and state taxes on current income.

9300 Provision for Federal Income Taxes.

9320 Provision for State Income Taxes.

9330 Provision for Local Income Taxes.

Part F. Land Development Costs Subsidiary Ledger

General Ledger Account 141

0100 Preacquisition Costs
0101 Options
0102 Fees
0103 Professional Services
0110 Acquisition Costs
0111 Purchase price undeveloped land
0112 Sales commissions
0113 Legal fees
0114 Appraisals
0115 Closing costs
0116 Interest and financing fees
0120 Land Planning and Design
0121 Bonds
0122 Fees
0123 Permits
0130 Engineering
0131 Civil engineering
0132 Soil testing
0133 Traffic engineering
0140 Earthwork

0141	Fill dirt		0165	Street signs
0142	Clearing lot		**0170**	**Signage**
0143	Rock removal		0171	Temporary
0144	Erosion control		0172	Permanent
0145	Dust control		**0180**	**Landscaping**
0150	**Utilities**		0181	Sod or seed
0151	Sewer lines		0182	Shrubs
0152	Storm sewer		0183	Trees
0153	Water lines		0184	Mulch
0154	Gas lines		0185	Other materials
0155	Electric lines		0186	Other labor
0156	Telephone lines		**0190**	**Amenities**
0157	Cable television lines		0191	Swimming pool
0160	**Streets and Walks**		0192	Tennis courts
0161	Curbs and gutters		0193	Tot lots
0162	Walkways		0194	Putting greens
0163	Paving		0195	Exercise trail
0164	Street lights			

Basic Accounts for Small-Volume Businesses

The following abbreviated list of accounts provides an example of the accounts typically used by small-volume builders who build under 25 units per year. Small-volume remodelers and developers can also adapt this group of basic accounts to their businesses. The complete NAHB Chart of Accounts shown in Appendices A and B contain more accounts than are normally required to perform the accounting function of a small construction firm. The listing below is a guide that small-volume builders may use to establish their own chart of accounts. The numerical codes and accounting categories listed are compatible with those used in the complete NAHB Chart of Accounts.

1000–1990   Assets
1000–1090   Cash
1010   Petty cash
1020   Cash on deposit, general
1040   Cash on deposit, savings and money market
1050   Cash on deposit, held in escrow

1100–1190   Short-term Investments
1110   Certificates of Deposit

1200–1290 Receivables

1210 Accounts receivable, trade
1230 Notes receivable

1400–1490 Construction Work in Progress

1420 Developed lots
1430 Direct construction cost
1450 Direct Construction cost—remodeling
1440 Indirect construction cost
1470 Cost in excess of billings

1600–1690 Other Current Assets

1610 Refundable deposits
1630 Employee advances
1660 Due from officers, stockholders, owners, or partners
1670 Deposits on plans
1690 Other current assets

1700–1790 Investments and Other Assets

1780 Organization cost

1800–1890 Property, Plant, and Equipment

1830 Office furniture and equipment
1840 Vehicles
1850 Construction equipment
1880 Leasehold improvements
1890 Computer equipment and software

1900–1990 Accumulated Depreciation

1930 Accumulated depreciation, office furniture and equipment
1940 Accumulated depreciation, vehicles
1950 Accumulated depreciation, construction equipment
1980 Accumulated depreciation, leasehold improvements
1990 Accumulated depreciation, computer equipment and software

2000–2990 Liabilities and Owners' Equity
2000–2090 Deposits by Customers

2010 Contract deposits

2100–2290 Accounts and Notes Payable

2110 Accounts payable, trade
2200 Line of credit payable
2230 Construction loans payable
2290 Notes payable, other

2300–2490 Other Current Liabilities

2310 Social Security and Medicare
2320 Federal payroll tax withheld and accrued
2330 State payroll tax withheld and accrued
2340 Other payroll withholdings
2420 Workers' Compensation insurance payable
2450 Due to officers, stockholders, owners, and partners
2490 Other current liabilities

2500–2890 Long-term Liabilities

2510 Long-term notes payable
2530 Mortgage notes payable
2620 Due to officers, stockholders, owners, long-term, and partners
2700 Other long-term liabilities

2900–2990 Owners' Equity

2900 Common stock
2920 Retained earnings
2950 Partnership or proprietorship account
2960 Distributions, dividends, and draws

3000–3990 Sales, Revenues, and Cost of Sales
3000–3490 Sales and Revenues

3050 Sales, developed lots
3110 Sales, single-family production
3120 Sales, single-family custom designed
3125 Sales, single family custom, no land
3130 Sales, residential remodeling
3190 Sales, other
3370 Design fees collected
3400 Miscellaneous income
3410 Interest income
3420 Dividend income
3450 Earned discounts
3490 Sales concessions and discounts

3500–3790 Cost of Sales

3550 Cost of sales, developed lots
3610 Cost of sales, single-family production
3620 Cost of sales, single-family custom designed
3625 Cost of sales, single family custom designed, no land
3630 Cost of sales, remodeling
3690 Cost of sales, other
3700 Direct construction cost for prior periods

3800–3899 Costs of Construction— Remodeling

3810   Direct labor
3820   Labor burden
3830   Building material
3840   Subcontractors
3850   Rental equipment
3860   Other direct construction costs
3870   Professional design fees

4000–4990   Indirect Construction Cost

4010   Construction salaries
4120   Workers' Compensation insurance
4265   Mobile phones, pagers, and radios
4410   Lease payments, construction vehicles
4420   Mileage reimbursement
4430   Repairs and maintenance, construction vehicles
4440   Operating expenses, construction vehicles
4450   Taxes, licenses, and insurance, construction vehicles
4510   Rent, construction equipment
4530   Repairs and maintenance, construction equipment
4540   Operating expenses, construction equipment
4550   Taxes and insurance, construction equipment
4560   Small tools and supplies
4610   Temporary utilities
4710   Warranty expenses
4990   Absorbed indirect costs

5000–5990   Financing Expenses

5020   Interest on notes payable
5040   Interest incurred on construction loans
5090   Interest expense, other
5120   Points and fees
5210   Closing costs

6000–6990   Sales and Marketing Expenses

6040   Sales commissions, in-house
6050   Sales commissions, outside
6310   Advertising
6330   Internet fees, web page design, and maintenance costs
6340   Brochures and catalogues
6350   Signs
6365   Promotions
6370   Agency commissions
6395   Referral fees

8000–8990   General and Administrative Expense

8010   Salaries, owners
8050   Salaries and wages, office and clerical
8110   Payroll taxes
8120   Workers' Compensation insurance
8130   Health and accident insurance
8140   Retirement, pension, and profit-sharing plans
8190   Other employee benefits
8210   Rent
8220   Office equipment rental
8230   Repairs and maintenance, administrative office space
8240   Repairs and maintenance, administrative office equipment
8250   Utilities, administrative office
8260   Telephone, administrative office
8270   Office supplies, administrative office
8280   Postage and deliveries
8290   Miscellaneous expenses, administrative office
8410   Lease, administrative vehicles
8420   Mileage reimbursement
8430   Repairs and maintenance, administration vehicles
8440   Operating expense, administration vehicles
8450   Taxes, licenses, and insurance, administration vehicles
8460   Travel
8470   Customer business expense
8520   Real estate taxes
8540   License fees
8590   Other taxes
8630   General liability insurance
8690   Other insurance
8710   Accounting services
8720   Legal services
8730   Consulting services
8770   Recruiting and hiring
8800   Depreciation expenses
8880   Amortization of organization cost
8910   Contributions
8911   Contributions, political

8920   Dues and subscriptions

8950   Bank charges

8960   Penalties

8990   Training and education expenses

9000–9990   Other Income and Expenses

9150   Gain or loss on sale of assets

9190   Other

9200   Extraordinary expenses

Basic Accounts for Remodelers

The following abbreviated list of accounts provides an example of the accounts typically used by remodelers. The complete NAHB Chart of Accounts shown in Appendices A and B contains more accounts than are normally required to perform the accounting function of the small construction firm. The listing below is a guide that remodelers may use to establish their own chart of accounts. The numerical codes and accounting categories listed are compatible with those used in the complete NAHB Chart of Accounts.

1000–1990   Assets
1010   Petty cash
1020   Cash on deposit, general
1030   Cash on deposit, payroll
1040   Cash on deposit, savings and money market
1210   Accounts receivable, trade
1230   Notes receivable
1280   Allowance for doubtful accounts
1290   Retentions (retainage) receivable
1310   Construction materials inventory

1330 Property held for remodeling
1470 Cost in excess of billings
1620 Prepaid expenses
1630 Employee advances
1650 Due from affiliated companies or subsidiaries
1660 Due from officers, stockholders, owners, or partners
1690 Other current assets
1780 Organization cost
1810 Land
1820 Buildings
1830 Office furniture and equipment
1840 Vehicles
1850 Construction equipment
1880 Leasehold improvements
1890 Computer equipment and software

1900–1990   Accumulated Depreciation
1920 Accumulated depreciation, buildings
1930 Accumulated depreciation, office furniture and equipment
1940 Accumulated depreciation, vehicles
1950 Accumulated depreciation, construction equipment
1980 Accumulated depreciation, leasehold improvements
1990 Accumulated depreciation, computer equipment and software

2000–2990   Liabilities and Owners' Equity
2010 Contract deposits
2110 Accounts payable, trade
2120 Retentions payable
2200 Line of credit payable
2240 Current portion of long-term debt
2290 Notes payable, other
2310 Social Security and Medicare
2320 Federal payroll tax withheld and accrued
2330 State payroll tax withheld and accrued
2410 Accrued commissions payable
2420 Workers' Compensation insurance payable
2425 Other accrued expenses
2440 Due to affiliated companies or subsidiaries
2450 Due to officers, stockholders, owners, and partners
2480 Billings in excess of costs
2490 Other current liabilities

2510 Long-term notes payable
2530 Mortgage notes payable
2700 Other long-term liabilities

2900–2990   Owners' Equity
2900 Common stock
2910 Additional paid in capital
2920 Retained earnings
2960 Distributions, dividends, and draws

3000–3990   Sales, Revenues, and Cost of Sales
3000–3490   Sales and Revenues
3130 Sales, residential remodeling
3133 Sales, commercial and industrial remodeling
3135 Sales, insurance restoration
3137 Sales, repairs
3190 Sales, other
3370 Design fees collected
3400 Miscellaneous income
3410 Interest income
3420 Dividend income
3450 Earned discounts

3800–3899 Costs of Construction— Remodeling
3810 Direct labor
3820 Labor burden
3830 Building material
3840 Subcontractors
3850 Rental equipment
3860 Other direct construction costs
3870 Professional design fees

4000–4990   Indirect Construction Cost
4030 Production manager
4040 Architects, drafters, estimators, and purchasers
4265 Mobile phones, pagers, and radios
4410 Lease payments, construction vehicles
4420 Mileage reimbursement
4430 Repairs and maintenance, construction vehicles
4440 Operating expenses, construction vehicles
4450 Taxes, licenses, and insurance, construction vehicles
4510 Rent, construction equipment
4530 Repairs and maintenance, construction equipment

4540 Operating expenses, construction equipment
4550 Taxes and insurance, construction equipment
4560 Small tools and supplies

4700 Warranty and Customer Service

5000–5990 Financing Expenses
5000–5090 Interest
5010 Interest on line of credit
5020 Interest on notes payable
5090 Interest expense, other

6000–6990 Sales and Marketing Expenses
6000–6090 Sales Salaries and Commissions
6010 Sales manager's compensation
6030 Salaries, sales personnel
6040 Sales commissions, in-house
6050 Sales commissions, outside

6100–6190 Payroll Taxes and Benefits, Sales and Marketing
6110 Payroll taxes, sales and marketing
6120 Workers' Compensation insurance, sales and marketing
6130 Health and accident insurance, sales and marketing
6140 Retirement, pension, and profit-sharing plans, sales and marketing
6190 Other benefits

6300–6390 Advertising and Sales Promotion
6310 Print advertising
6320 Radio advertising
6325 Television advertising
6330 Internet fees, web page design, and maintenance costs
6340 Brochures and catalogues
6350 Signs
6355 Billboards
6365 Promotions
6370 Agency commissions
6390 Public relations
6395 Referral fees
6700–6790 Sales and Marketing Fees
6710 Market research and consultation
6720 Interior design fee

6770 Recruiting fees and expenses, sales and marketing personnel
6780 Training and education expenses

8000–8990 General and Administrative Expense
8010 Salaries, owners
8050 Salaries and wages, office and clerical
8110 Payroll taxes
8120 Workers' Compensation insurance
8130 Health and accident insurance
8140 Retirement, pension, and profit-sharing plans
8190 Other employee benefits
8210 Rent
8220 Office equipment, rental
8230 Repairs and maintenance, administrative office space
8240 Repairs and maintenance, administrative office equipment
8250 Utilities
8260 Telephone
8270 Office supplies
8280 Postage and deliveries
8300 Computer expenses
8410 Lease, vehicles
8420 Mileage reimbursement
8430 Repairs and maintenance, vehicles
8440 Operating expense, vehicles
8450 Taxes, licenses, and insurance,-administration vehicles
8460 Travel
8470 Customer business expense
8480 Meeting expenses
8530 Personal property taxes
8540 License fees
8590 Other taxes
8610 Hazard insurance/property insurance
8630 General liability insurance
8690 Other insurance
8710 Accounting services
8720 Legal services
8730 Consulting services
8770 Recruiting and hiring
8800 Depreciation expenses
8880 Amortization of organization cost
8900 Bad debts
8910 Contributions

8911   Contributions, political
8920   Dues and subscriptions
8950   Bank charges
8960   Penalties
8990   Training and education expenses

9000–9990   Other Income and Expenses
9100–9190   Other Income
9150   Gain or loss on sale of assets
9190   Other

9200–9290   Other Expenses
9200   Extraordinary Expenses

Direct Construction Costs, Subsidiary Ledger

General Ledger Account 1430

1000–1999   Preparation Preliminaries

1010   Building permits
1020   HBA assessments
1030   Warranty fees
1110   Blueprints
1120   Surveys
1210   Lot clearing
1220   Fill dirt and material
1230   Rough grading
1300   Demolition
1400   Temporary electric
1420   Individual wells
1430   Water service
1440   Septic system
1450   Sewer system
1460   Gas service
1470   Electric service

1480 Telephone service
1490 Other utility connections

2000–2999   Excavation and Foundation
2000 Excavation and back fill
2100 Footings and foundation
2110 Rebar and reinforcing steel
2120 Concrete block
2130 Window wells
2200 Waterproofing
2300 Termite protection

3000–3999   Rough Structure
3100 Structural steel
3110 Lumber—1st package
3120 Lumber—2nd package
3130 Lumber—3rd package
3140 Trusses
3150 Miscellaneous lumber
3210 Framing labor—draw #1
3220 Framing labor—draw #2
3230 Framing labor—draw #3
3300 Windows
3350 Skylights
3400 Exterior siding
3410 Exterior trim labor
3500 Flatwork material
3550 Flatwork labor
3610 HVAC—rough
3620 HVAC—final
3710 Plumbing—ground
3720 Plumbing—rough
3730 Plumbing—final
3810 Electrical—rough
3820 Electrical—final
3910 Gutters and downspout

4000–4999   Full Enclosure
4100 Roofing material
4150 Roofing labor
4200 Masonry material
4250 Masonry labor
4300 Exterior doors
4350 Garage door
4400 Insulation
4500 Fireplaces

5000–5999   Finishing Trades
5100 Drywall
5200 Interior trim material
5250 Interior trim labor
5300 Painting
5400 Cabinets and vanities
5450 Countertops
5510 Ceramic tile
5520 Special flooring
5530 Vinyl
5540 Carpet
5610 Hardware
5620 Shower doors and mirrors
5630 Appliances
5700 Electrical fixtures
5810 Wall coverings
5890 Special finishes

6000–6999   Completion and Inspection
6100 Clean-up
6200 Final grade
6300 Driveways
6400 Patios and walks
6450 Decks
6490 Fences
6500 Ornamental iron
6600 Landscaping
6700 Pools

Indirect Construction Costs, Subsidiary Ledger

General Ledger Account 1440

4000–4090 Salaries and Wages
4010   Superintendents
4020   Laborers
4030   Production manager
4040   Architects, drafters, estimators, and purchasers
4050   Other indirect construction wages

4100–4190 Payroll Taxes and Benefits
4110   Payroll taxes
4120   Workers' Compensation insurance
4130   Health and accident insurance
4140   Retirement, pension, and profit sharing
4150   Union benefits
4190   Other benefits

4200–4290   Field Office Expenses

4210   Rent, field office
4230   Repairs and maintenance, field office
4250   Utilities, field office
4260   Telephone, field office
4265   Mobile phones, pagers, and radios
4290   Other field office expenses

4300–4390   Field Warehouse and Storage Expenses

4310   Rent, field warehouse and storage
4330   Repairs and maintenance, field warehouse and storage
4350   Utilities, field warehouse and storage
4360   Telephone, field warehouse and storage

4400–4490   Construction Vehicles, Travel, and Entertainment

4410   Lease payments, construction vehicles
4420   Mileage reimbursement
4430   Repairs and maintenance, construction vehicles
4440   Operating expenses, construction vehicles
4450   Taxes, licenses, and insurance, construction vehicles
4460   Travel, construction department
4470   Customer business entertainment, construction
4480   Training and education, construction
4490   Recruiting fees and expenses, construction

4500–4590   Construction Equipment

4510   Rent, construction equipment

4530   Repairs and maintenance, construction equipment
4540   Operating expenses, construction equipment
4550   Taxes and insurance, construction equipment
4560   Small tools and supplies

4600–4690   Expenses for Maintaining Unsold Units and Units Under Construction

4610   Temporary utilities
4620   Trash maintenance
4640   Lawn care
4650   Utilities, completed units
4660   Repairs and maintenance, completed units

4700–4790   Warranty and Customer Service

4710   Salaries and wages, warranty
4720   Material, warranty
4730   Subcontractor, warranty
4790   Other, warranty expenses

4800–4890   Depreciation Expenses

4820   Depreciation, construction office
4830   Depreciation, warehouse
4840   Depreciation, construction vehicles
4850   Depreciation, construction equipment

4900–4990   Other

4910   Insurance and bonding expenses
4920   Builders risk insurance
4990   Absorbed indirect costs

APPENDIX G

Land Development Costs, Subsidiary Ledger

General Ledger Account 1410

0100 Pre-acquisition Costs
0101 Options
0102 Fees
0103 Professional services

0110 Acquisition Costs
0111 Purchase price, undeveloped land
0112 Sales commissions
0113 Legal fees
0114 Appraisals
0115 Closing costs
0116 Interest and financial fees

0120 Land Planning and Design
0121 Bonds
0122 Fees
0123 Permits

0130 Engineering
0131 Civil engineering
0132 Soil testing
0133 Traffic engineering

0140 Earthwork
0141 Fill dirt
0142 Clearing lot
0143 Rock removal
0144 Erosion control
0145 Dust control

0150 Utilities
0151 Sewer lines
0152 Storm sewer
0153 Water lines
0154 Gas lines
0155 Electric lines
0156 Telephone lines
0157 Cable television lines
0158 Special technology lines

0160 Streets and Walks
0161 Curbs and gutters

0162 Walkways
0163 Paving
0164 Street lights
0165 Street signs

0170 Signage
0171 Temporary
0172 Entry sign
0173 Permanent signs

0180 Landscaping
0181 Sod or seed
0182 Shrubs
0183 Trees
0184 Mulch
0185 Other materials
0186 Labor

0190 Amenities
0191 Swimming pool
0192 Tennis court
0193 Tot lots
0194 Putting greens
0195 Exercise trail

Index

Page numbers in *italics* refer to illustrations

Cash
   custodianship of, 38
   daily requirements, 55
   disbursements of, 25, 41–42, 54–55
   management of, 39
   petty, 42
   withdrawals of, 40
Cash accounting, 22
Cash balance
   cash flow analysis using, 54–56
   control of, 39–41
   description of, 25
Cash flow
   analysis of, 54–56
   report regarding, 88, 89
Cash receipts, 24–25, 41–42, 54, 98
Certified public accountant
   accountant vs., 3
   audits by, 5–6
   compilations by, 6
   definition of, 3
   firms, 5
   interactions with, 5
   reviews by, 6
   selection of, 5
Change orders, 79
Chart of accounts
   complete list of, 106–123
   customizing of, 29
   description of, 27–28
   developers, 73–74
   direct construction costs, 92, 132–133
   indirect construction costs, 93, 134–135
   land acquisition and development costs, 73–74, 136–137
   loan administration, 43
   multiproject companies, 70
   numerical coding system for, 28–29
   outline of, 99–105
   remodeling operations, 79, 128–131
   small-volume businesses, 124–127
Check(s)
   numerical sequence of, 40
   signing of, 40–42
   voided, 40
Check register
   definition of, 39
   reconciliation of, 40–41
Closing entries, 35
Coding, for chart of accounts, 28–29
Compilations, 6
Completed contract accounting, 23

Computer(s)
   accounting applications completed using, 66–68
   application service provider system, 67–68
   computer-aided design programs, 68
   data processing using, 8, 31, 65–66
   databases, 67–68
   Internet capabilities, 67
   password protection, 38
   remote access to, 67
   server-based, 67
   software, 3, 67–68
   subsidiary ledger entries, 31
   tips for purchasing, 67
   word processing applications, 68
Computer-aided design, 68
Construction costs
   budgeting for, 82–84
   direct, *See* Direct construction costs
   indirect, *See* Indirect construction costs
   remodeling operations, 79
Contracts, 22
Controlling, 2
Cost(s)
   carrying, 92
   construction, *See* Direct construction costs; Indirect construction costs
   direct, 15
   estimating of, 43
   expenses vs., 25
   fixed, 25
   flowchart for, *17,* 30
   indirect, 15
   internal control, 39
   land acquisition and development, *See* Land acquisition and development costs
   variable, 25–26
Cost codes accounts, 63
Cost of sales
   construction costs, 48–49
   description of, 30
   gross profits affected by, 53
   reductions in, 53–54
Cost recovery method of revenue recognition, 98
Costing
   absorption, 24, 49
   definition of, 23
   direct, 23
CPA, *See* Certified public accountant
Credit approval, 79
Credits, 11–12, 14
Current ratio, 56
Custodianship, 38